QUESTIONS

VOLUME **4**

101 Bizarre and Cool Q&As

Melina Gerosa Bellows

BRIGHT MATTER BOOKS

New York

Contents

About how long does it take a **spider** to build a web?

a. less than one day

b. one week

c. one month

ANSWER: a

less than one day

MOST SPIDERS THAT MAKE WHEEL-SHAPED WEBS CAN DO IT IN ABOUT TWO HOURS, THOUGH IT VARIES FROM SPECIES TO SPECIES. Webs are made up of a fine material called spider silk, which consists of natural protein fibers made inside a spider's body. Some spider silk, such as the silk made by orb weaver spiders, is as strong as steel. Spiders are able to produce seven different kinds of silk that can be used to support objects, as shelter, and even as parachutes. **These spiderweb parachutes are used in a process called ballooning, which is when spiders release silk that catches the wind and allows them to move through the air.** Spiders also use their silk in a method called **dragline.** This is when a spider attaches a line of silk to its web like an anchor. If the spider falls from its web, it uses this anchor as a way to climb back up.

Instant Genius
Golden silk orb weaver spiders spin webs that look like they're made of gold.

Golden Silk Orb Weaver Spider

True or False:

The Declaration of Independence was hidden during World War II.

IN CONGRESS, JULY 4, 1776.

unanimous Declaration of the thirteen united States of A

When in the Course of human events, it becomes necessary for one people to dissolve the political bands which have conne the earth, the separate and equal station to which the Laws of Nature and of Nature's God entitle them, a decent respect to the opini impel them to the separation. — We hold these truths to be self-evident, that all men are created equal, th that among these are Life, Liberty and the pursuit of Happiness. — That to secure these rights, Governments are institut — That whenever any Form of Government becomes destructive of these ends, it is the Right of the People to alter or to on such principles and organizing its powers in such form, as to them shall seem most likely to effect their Safety a should not be changed for light and transient causes; and accordingly all experience hath shewn, th forms to which they are accustomed. But when a long train of abuses and to throw off such Government, and to provide

11

AFTER PEARL HARBOR WAS ATTACKED BY THE JAPANESE ON DECEMBER 7, 1941, the government of the United States decided they needed to hide the original copies of the Declaration of Independence and the U.S. Constitution because Washington, D.C., was under threat of attack. **During the night, military personnel took these important documents by train to a secret location— the Fort Knox army base in Kentucky.** The documents remained at Fort Knox until 1944.

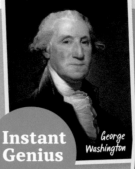

George Washington

James Madison

Instant Genius

Two signers of the U.S. Constitution later became U.S. presidents. They were George Washington and James Madison.

NOW YOU KNOW!

President Abraham Lincoln's Gettysburg Address was another document secretly sent to Fort Knox at the same time as the Declaration of Independence and the Constitution.

Fort Knox, Kentucky

What's the difference between white and black **watermelon seeds?**

a. There is no difference.

b. The black ones are older.

c. The white ones are edible and the black ones are not.

ANSWER: **b**

The black ones are older.

WHEN DIGGING YOUR TEETH INTO A SWEET SLICE OF WATERMELON, YOU MAY HAVE NOTICED THAT THERE ARE BOTH WHITE AND BLACK SEEDS. The only difference between these seeds is their age. **The longer the seeds grow inside the fruit, the harder and darker they get.** When a watermelon is harvested, the growing stops, and a very small percentage of its seeds remain undeveloped. These are the white seeds. **If you plant the dark seeds in the ground, they can grow into a new watermelon plant.** If you plant the white seeds, they won't grow. Both white and dark seeds are edible, although the dark ones are more fun to spit out!

Instant Genius
There are between 200 and 800 seeds in a watermelon.

The color of a hen's eggs depend on its feathers.

#4

A female chicken isn't called a hen until she can lay eggs. Until then, female chickens are called pullets.

Chicken's earlobe

ANSWER: **False**

Instant Genius

There are about 69 billion chickens on Earth (and about 7.8 billion people).

HENS ARE ADULT FEMALE CHICKENS, AND ONLY FEMALE CHICKENS LAY EGGS. The color of a hen's eggs often depend on the color of her earlobes. For example, the breed of chickens known as Araucanas have green or blue earlobes, and they lay bluish or greenish eggs. **Hens with white earlobes, such as the Andalusian chicken from Spain, also lay white eggs, but it's hens with red earlobes that break this pattern: They lay brown eggs.** It takes about 26 hours for an egg to fully develop inside a hen, so hens usually lay only one egg a day.

Why are so many people right-handed?

a. because that's the way they learned to write

b. The brain is wired that way.

c. because they don't practice with their left hands

NOW YOU KNOW!
Identical twins don't always share the same dominant hand. Sometimes one twin can be left-handed and the other can be right-handed.

ANSWER: b

The brain is wired that way.

ACCORDING TO STATISTICS, ABOUT 90 PERCENT OF THE POPULATION IS RIGHT-HANDED. The other 10 percent is either left-handed or ambidextrous. This is true of cultures all over the world. Which hand you use to do things like write and eat actually starts in the brain, not the hand. **The right hand is controlled by the left side of the brain, and vice versa.** Some scientists think that most people are right-handed because language is rooted in the left side of the brain. **They believe that when language was first developing 600,000 years ago, right-handedness came along simply as a side effect of the brain activity. According to one study, there is a link between left-handedness and being a genius.** Famous lefties include Barack Obama, Aristotle, Mozart, and Marie Curie. It was a myth that Albert Einstein was left-handed.

Instant Genius
Some people are ambidextrous, meaning they can use both hands equally.

18

Spacecraft

#6

have flown by all
the other planets
in our solar system.

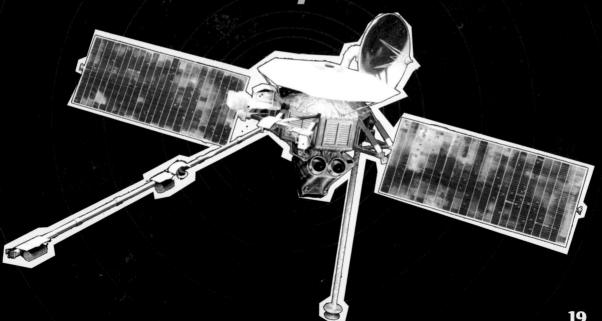

NOW YOU KNOW!
The two Voyager spacecraft are still flying. They are now in a very distant area known as interstellar space, where the sun's magnetic field can no longer reach.

Voyager 1

ANSWER: True

IN 1977, NASA LAUNCHED TWO VOYAGER SPACECRAFTS: VOYAGER 1 AND VOYAGER 2. For more than 40 years, these spacecraft have been sending scientists lots of information about space. **They have also flown by Jupiter, Saturn, Uranus, and Neptune.** The first spacecraft to visit Mercury was Mariner 10, launched in 1974. It sent back the first pictures of the planet's surface. **Numerous spacecraft have also flown by Venus and Mars.** Robotic vehicles called rovers have even landed on Mars to explore its surface.

Chinese Zhurong rover

Instant Genius
The most recent rover to land on Mars was the Chinese Zhurong rover, which landed in May 2021.

Why did the ancient Egyptians

7

Egyptians
fill their tombs with treasures?

a. **to bribe the gods**

b. **to use in the afterlife**

c. **to prevent people from stealing them**

Luxor, Egypt

ANSWER: b

to use in the afterlife

THE ANCIENT EGYPTIANS BELIEVED THAT DEATH WAS THE BEGINNING OF THE AFTERLIFE, AND THAT IN THE AFTERLIFE, THEY WOULD NEED USE OF THEIR BODIES. This is why they were mummified. **As part of this long process, all organs except the heart were removed and preserved in special jars.** The heart was left in the mummy's body to be weighed in the afterlife, as it was thought this would determine if a person led a good life. The ancient Egyptians also believed that they could take with them and use their earthly possessions. **Tombs of the rich were packed with expensive jewelry, boats, chariots, and weapons.** Even tombs of the poor had a few precious items such as food, water, and good luck charms.

Dolphins

#8

**sometimes ask
humans for help.**

THERE HAVE BEEN SEVERAL REPORTS OF DOLPHINS RESCUING HUMANS AT SEA, including stories about pods of dolphins surrounding groups of swimmers to protect them in the water. **What may be more surprising is a true tale of how a dolphin named Notch swam up to divers to signal for help.** The divers were swimming with manta rays in Hawaii when one of them noticed that the dolphin had a hook stuck between its mouth and its pectoral fin. **The diver used his fingers to remove the hook while Notch patiently waited.** Then, the dolphin went to the surface to take a breath before returning to let the divers check him one more time. **Scientists can't explain how dolphins know how to help, or ask for help.**

Indo-Pacific bottlenose dolphins

NOW YOU KNOW!
The Amazon River is home to three species of freshwater dolphins, including the pink river dolphin.

Pink river dolphin

What is the only part of the **human body** that can't repair itself?

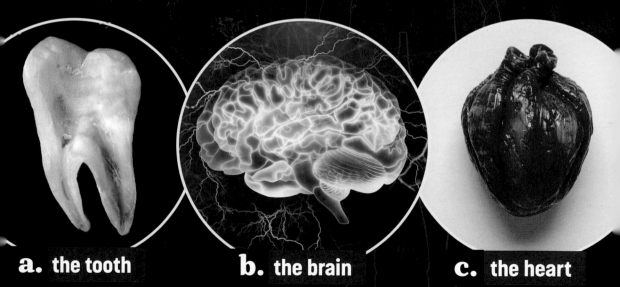

a. the tooth   **b.** the brain   **c.** the heart

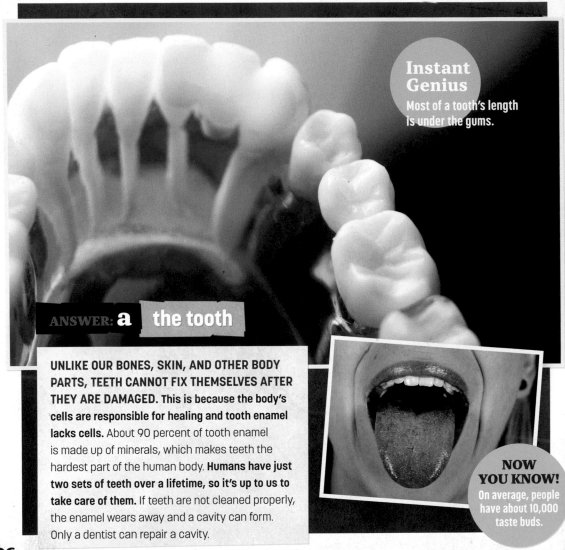

ANSWER: a the tooth

UNLIKE OUR BONES, SKIN, AND OTHER BODY PARTS, TEETH CANNOT FIX THEMSELVES AFTER THEY ARE DAMAGED. **This is because the body's cells are responsible for healing and tooth enamel lacks cells.** About 90 percent of tooth enamel is made up of minerals, which makes teeth the hardest part of the human body. **Humans have just two sets of teeth over a lifetime, so it's up to us to take care of them.** If teeth are not cleaned properly, the enamel wears away and a cavity can form. Only a dentist can repair a cavity.

Which **language** has the most words for snow?

#10

c. Scots

a. Inuktitut

b. Swedish

Snowball fight!

NOW YOU KNOW! Japanese macaque monkeys have been observed making and playing with snowballs.

ANSWER: C **Scots**

ACCORDING TO A STUDY AT THE UNIVERSITY OF GLASGOW IN SCOTLAND, THE LANGUAGE THAT CONTAINS THE MOST WORDS FOR SNOW—OVER 400—IS SCOTS. The reason is because the weather in Scotland greatly affects how people live there, so they have developed a large vocabulary to describe and communicate. **These words include different categories of snow, descriptions of snowflakes, different ways that snow can move, and clothing meant to be worn in the snow.** There's even a Scottish word to describe a ghost seen in the snow: *snaw-ghast*. **Inuit dialects have about 50 words for snow, and the Swedish language has a solid 25.**

Instant Genius
Snow isn't white— it's translucent.

28

How many varieties of **pumpkin** are there?

a. 10

b. 45

c. 56

NOW YOU KNOW!
Ohio was home to the largest pumpkin pie ever baked. It weighed 3,699 pounds (1,678 kg) and was 20 feet (6 m) in diameter.

ANSWER: b 45

Instant Genius

In Australia and New Zealand, blue pumpkins are popular for baking and cooking.

PUMPKINS ARE IN THE GOURD AND SQUASH FAMILY. There are 45 varieties of pumpkins, and some have fun names, including Jackpot, Big Moon, Triple Treat, Sweetie Pie, Baby Boo, and Funny Face. Pumpkins have been grown for thousands of years and are usually orange, but they can also come in tan, red, yellow, green, white, and even blue. **Although we think of these colorful edibles as veggies, a pumpkin is actually a fruit because it grows from a flowering plant that produces seeds that are protected by the fruit.** (Vegetables are different because the parts we eat are the leaves, stems, and roots.)

Which statement is not true about Michelle Obama?

a. She was the first African American First Lady.

b. She got her law degree from Harvard University.

c. President Barack Obama was her mentor when she first practiced law.

ANSWER: **C**

President Barack Obama was her mentor when she first practiced law.

MICHELLE OBAMA WAS THE FIRST AFRICAN AMERICAN FIRST LADY AND RECEIVED HER LAW DEGREE FROM HARVARD LAW SCHOOL. She is married to Barack Obama, the 44th president and the first African American president of the United States. However, she and Barack first met at a Chicago law firm, when *she* became *his* mentor. **During her eight years in the White House, Michelle Obama was an advocate for children and the African American community. She created programs supporting military families and encouraging children to eat healthy foods and exercise.** She also created a community service program to encourage young people to become volunteers. In 2018, she released an autobiography about her life and her time as First Lady.

Tigers and house cats share 95.6 percent of their DNA.

Roar!

Hiss!

Instant Genius

Because of habitat loss and conflicts with humans, there are only about 4,000 tigers left in the wild.

ANSWER: **True**

SCIENTISTS DISCOVERED THAT YOUR KITTEN MAY HAVE MORE IN COMMON WITH A WILD TIGER THAN YOU THOUGHT. A common ancestor of house cats and tigers lived 10.8 million years ago. This is why they have so many similarities. **Both have five toes on their front paws and four on their back paws, a characteristic that makes them fast and silent runners.** They have a great sense of smell, flexible spines designed for hunting, and spend 30 to 50 percent of their time grooming. House cats and tigers both mark their territory with urine, too.

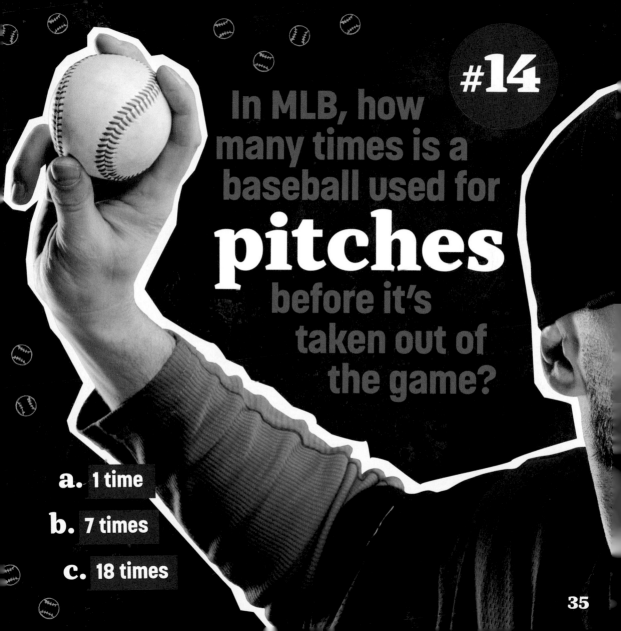

#14

In MLB, how many times is a baseball used for **pitches** before it's taken out of the game?

a. 1 time

b. 7 times

c. 18 times

ANSWER: b **7 times**

THE AVERAGE LIFE SPAN OF A BASEBALL IN THE MAJOR LEAGUES IS SHORT. Each ball is used for a few plays, or about seven pitches, before the ball is retired. Why? Scuffed, dirty, or damaged balls could impact the way a ball moves when it's in the air. **While each baseball is used for only a few plays, a lot of effort goes into making each one. Baseballs contain a cork at the center called a "pill."** A machine tightly wraps the pill with 316 yards (289 m) of wool. These layers are then wrapped in cowhide. **Finally, each ball gets 108 hand stitches with red cotton thread. Then, they are ready for play!**

True or False:

It's impossible for **one city** to be on two separate continents.

#15

37

The Grand Bazaar, Istanbul

NOW YOU KNOW!
The Grand Bazaar in Istanbul, operating since 1461, is one of the oldest and largest covered markets in the world. It has 5,000 stalls and stretches over 60 streets.

ANSWER: **False**

THE ONLY CITY IN THE WORLD THAT SITS ON TWO CONTINENTS IS ISTANBUL, TURKEY. One part of the city lies in Europe and the other part lies in Asia. **These two areas are separated by the natural boundary of the Bosporus, a 19-mile-long (30 km) waterway that connects the Black Sea with the Sea of Marmara.** Istanbul is thousands of years old and has been the capital of three ancient empires—the Roman, the Byzantine, and the Ottoman.

Mount Ararat, Turkey

Instant Genius
Turkey's highest mountain, Mount Ararat, has two peaks!

#16

Where was the world's first known flushing toilet?

a. **Greece**

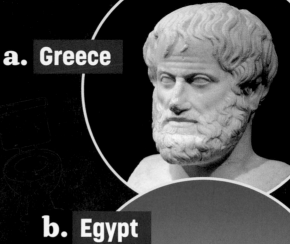

b. **Egypt**

c. **Kenya**

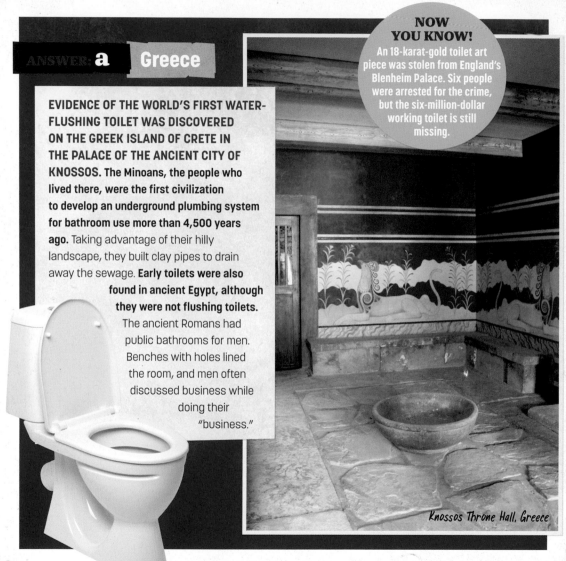

EVIDENCE OF THE WORLD'S FIRST WATER-FLUSHING TOILET WAS DISCOVERED ON THE GREEK ISLAND OF CRETE IN THE PALACE OF THE ANCIENT CITY OF KNOSSOS. The Minoans, the people who lived there, were the first civilization to develop an underground plumbing system for bathroom use more than 4,500 years ago. Taking advantage of their hilly landscape, they built clay pipes to drain away the sewage. **Early toilets were also found in ancient Egypt, although they were not flushing toilets.** The ancient Romans had public bathrooms for men. Benches with holes lined the room, and men often discussed business while doing their "business."

Knossos Throne Hall, Greece

#17

The cutting board

is probably the dirtiest surface in your house.

41

ANSWER: **True**

ACCORDING TO A NEW STUDY, A TYPICAL CUTTING BOARD IS LIKELY ONE OF THE DIRTIEST SURFACES IN THE HOME. **It's 200 times dirtier than a toilet seat, with a whopping average bacteria count of 24,250 per 0.15 square inches (1 sq cm).** When food is cut with a knife, the little gouges left in the cutting board surface provide the perfect environment for germs to fester. **These tiny microorganisms can cause food poisoning that upsets the stomach.** Other places in the house that harbor germs include the bathroom faucet handles, the kitchen sponge, the carpet, the pet's food bowl, and the TV remote.

True or False:

Earthworms
have eyes.

Where's the garden?

#18

43

Zophobas morio

Flour worms

Mealworms

ANSWER: **False**

THERE ARE 2,700 TYPES OF EARTHWORMS, BUT NONE HAVE EYES. However, an earthworm can tell light from dark because a worm's front end has receptors that can sense light. Earthworms also do not have ears, but they can sense movement around them through vibrations. **Earthworms eat decaying material such as plants and dead animals and require a lot of moisture, because if they dry out completely, they will die.** This is why worms burrow so deep into the ground to where the soil is moist.

Instant Genius
Earthworms have five hearts.

African night crawler

What color can make you feel hungry?

a. red

b. blue

c. yellow

ANSWER: a   red

HAVE YOU EVER NOTICED THAT A LOT OF FOOD COMPANIES USE THE COLOR RED ON THEIR SIGNS AND PACKAGING? The reason may be more than just how it looks. **According to research, red is the color most likely to induce hunger.** Many people associate the color with warmth and positive memories. **This can make us feel energetic, which can lead to burning calories, which can then make us hungry.** Some scientists believe red and yellow together can make us even hungrier, an idea some experts call the "ketchup and mustard theory," which can make us even hungrier.

How many words are in the average eight-year-old's vocabulary?

a. 3,000

b. 8,000

c. 10,000

#20

ENGLISH DICTIONARY

ANSWER: **C**

10,000

CHILDREN LEARN WORDS VERY QUICKLY, AND SPEAKING WITH OLDER PEOPLE AND OVERHEARING OLDER PEOPLE SPEAK ARE TWO WAYS THEY PICK UP WORDS. According to a recent survey, the average one-year-old knows 50 words, the **average five-year-old knows 5,000 words, and the average eight-year-old knows 10,000 words.** Vocabulary growth usually stops in middle age, and most adults know about 42,000 words. **English has the largest vocabulary of all languages with about 800,000 words.**

THE

Instant Genius
"The" is the most commonly used word in the English language.

It's possible to **tickle** yourself.

#21

ANSWER: **False**

THE ELEMENT OF SURPRISE IS THE KEY INGREDIENT TO FEELING A TICKLE. The reason you can't tickle yourself is because the cerebellum, an area in the back of your brain, keeps track of movement. When you attempt to tickle yourself, your brain predicts the oncoming sensation and is prepared for it. **This avoids the element of surprise, so you don't feel ticklish.** When someone else tickles you, your brain doesn't know it's coming, so the tickle makes you laugh. Some people are so ticklish, they will start laughing before anyone even touches them!

Instant Genius
Chimpanzees have been observed tickling each other.

50

Why do icebergs float?

a. because they're in saltwater

b. because they're denser than water

c. because they're made of fresh water

Arctic Icebergs

ANSWER: C

because they're made of fresh water

ICEBERGS ARE PIECES OF ICE THAT FLOAT ON A BODY OF WATER SUCH AS AN OCEAN, but they form on land. Icebergs are created when chunks of ice break off from larger icebergs, glaciers, or ice shelves. **They can be found floating in the Arctic, North Atlantic, and Southern Oceans.** To be considered an iceberg, the ice must be more than 16 feet (5 m) above the surface of the water. **It also needs to be between 98 and 164 feet (30 and 50 m) thick and take up a space of at least 5,400 square feet (502 sq m). The tip that you see is only about 10 percent of the iceberg; the rest of it is actually underwater.** Icebergs float because they are made of fresh water, which is less dense than the salt water they are sitting in. Because water expands as it freezes, ice has more volume and takes up more space than seawater.

#23

Humans

can outlast almost any animal in a long-distance race.

ANSWER: True

Instant Genius
The pronghorn antelope can run at a top speed of almost 60 miles an hour (97 kmh), making it the fastest land animal over long distances.

WHEN IT COMES TO SPRINTING, ANIMALS HAVE AN ADVANTAGE OVER HUMANS. Why? Most animals have four legs, which gives them double muscle power for short bursts of speed, which is essential when outrunning a predator. **When it comes to running long distances, however, humans can outlast other mammals.** This is because the human body is better at keeping itself from overheating. **When mammals are hot, the primary way they cool off is by panting—quickly exchanging hot air from their lungs with cool outside air. But humans, on the other hand, cool down by sweating.** When the sweat evaporates off the skin, the body cools down. This enables humans to stay cooler and run farther than animals, which have to stop because they are overheating.

How fast can a raindrop fall?

a. up to 1 mile an hour (1.6 kmh)

b. up to 5 miles an hour (8 kmh)

c. up to 20 miles an hour (32 kmh)

ANSWER: C

up to 20 miles an hour (32 kmh)

A RAINDROP IS BORN IN A CLOUD. The two clouds that most commonly make rain are nimbostratus and cumulonimbus. When the raindrop grows heavier than the surrounding air in the cloud, gravity pulls the water drop from the cloud to Earth. As it falls, air friction slows its motion. This evens out in a constant speed called terminal velocity. Larger drops fall faster than smaller drops. Big raindrops, which are about the size of a housefly, can fall up to 20 miles per hour (32 kmh). Smaller raindrops, which are the size of a flea, travel around 2 miles per hour (3 kmh). **Depending on the size, it takes about two minutes for a raindrop to fall from a cloud to the ground. Every minute, 1 billion tons of rain falls to Earth.**

Instant Genius

Raindrops are not shaped like teardrops; instead, they are flattened like a jelly bean as they fall.

Genius scientist
Stephen Hawking
struggled as a student.

#25

57

Stephen Hawking, Cambridge Film Festival

GALILEO GALILEI

ANSWER: **True**

BRITISH PHYSICIST STEPHEN HAWKING, WHO WAS CONSIDERED A GENIUS, ADMITTED THAT HE STRUGGLED AS A STUDENT. **He didn't learn to read properly until age eight and was behind in school.** But he was very intelligent and had many other interests, including stars in the night sky. Hawking went on to graduate at the top of his high school class and attend the University of Oxford in England. **By age 21, Hawking was diagnosed with a disease called ALS, which affected his muscles. He wasn't expected to live more than a few years, but he defied the odds, living until he was 76 and becoming a scientist at the forefront of astrophysics.** Eventually, Hawking was confined to a wheelchair and could no longer speak. He communicated through a special computer that spoke for him. The computer allowed him to "type" words using his cheek muscles and would then say the words for him. Hawking spent his life studying the relationship between space and time and made many contributions to our understanding of the universe.

About what percentage of people have 20/20 vision?

a. one-third

b. two-thirds

c. three-fourths

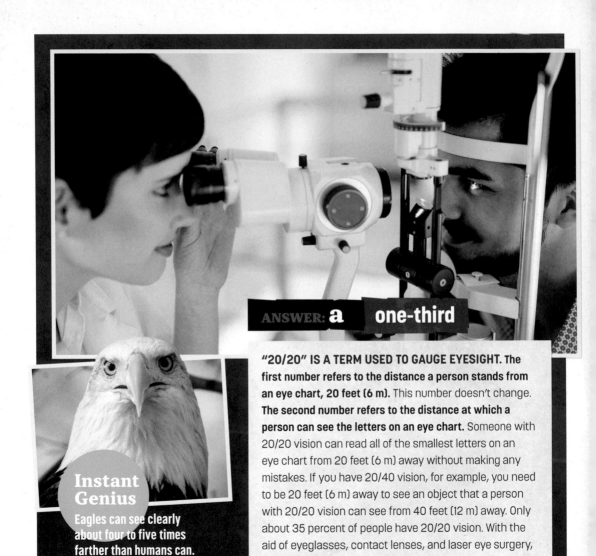

Instant Genius

Eagles can see clearly about four to five times farther than humans can.

"20/20" IS A TERM USED TO GAUGE EYESIGHT. The first number refers to the distance a person stands from an eye chart, 20 feet (6 m). This number doesn't change. **The second number refers to the distance at which a person can see the letters on an eye chart.** Someone with 20/20 vision can read all of the smallest letters on an eye chart from 20 feet (6 m) away without making any mistakes. If you have 20/40 vision, for example, you need to be 20 feet (6 m) away to see an object that a person with 20/20 vision can see from 40 feet (12 m) away. Only about 35 percent of people have 20/20 vision. With the aid of eyeglasses, contact lenses, and laser eye surgery, that number increases to 75 percent.

27

True or False:

Olympic gold medals are made of pure gold.

Anna Schaffelhuber, Germany

NOW YOU KNOW!
Special "bonus" medals containing fragments from a meteor that had exploded over Russia were given to 10 gold medal winners at the 2014 Sochi Games.

ANSWER: False

WHEN THE MODERN OLYMPIC GAMES BEGAN IN 1896, AFTER A 1,500-YEAR BREAK, WINNERS STARTED TO RECEIVE GOLD MEDALS. However, no solid gold medals have been given out since the 1912 Stockholm Games. These days, gold medals are 92.5 percent silver and plated with gold on top. Each gold medal contains 6 grams of gold, valued at around $349, and 394 grams of sterling silver, worth about $323.

Instant Genius

Winners at the first Olympic Games, which started in the eighth century BC, received wreaths made of olive leaves.

You can fry an **egg** on the sidewalk.

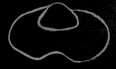

ANSWER: False

IN ORDER TO FRY AN EGG, THE TEMPERATURE WOULD NEED TO BE AT LEAST 158° F (70° C) TO COOK THE PROTEIN IN THE EGG. Concrete only gets to 145° F (63° C), which is plenty hot on bare feet but not hot enough to completely fry an egg. Compared to metal, concrete is a poor conductor of heat and therefore not an ideal substance for frying. Also, the wetness of the egg slightly cools the pavement. But this doesn't stop people from trying to do this. In fact, July 4 is Sidewalk Egg Frying Day.

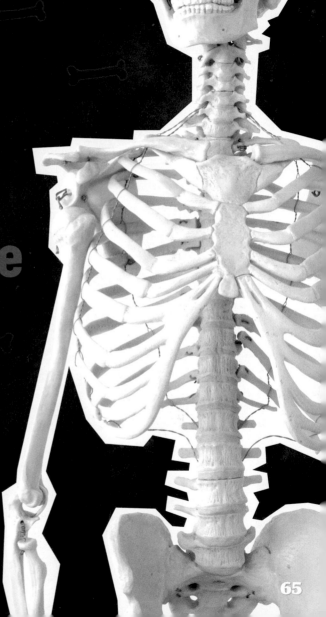

#29

True or False:

Some people are born with an **extra rib.**

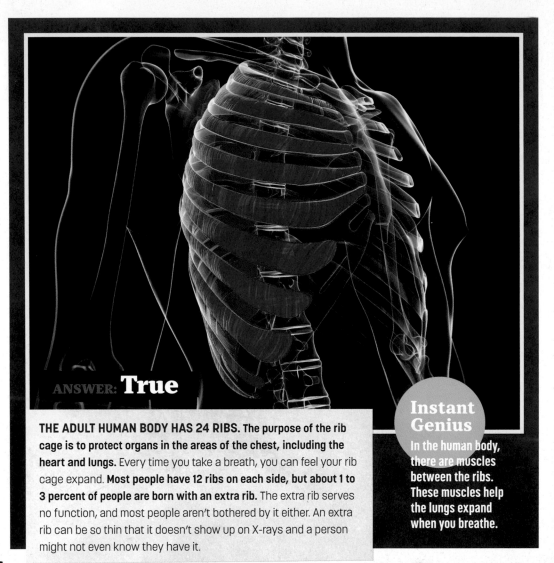

ANSWER: **True**

THE ADULT HUMAN BODY HAS 24 RIBS. The purpose of the rib cage is to protect organs in the areas of the chest, including the **heart and lungs.** Every time you take a breath, you can feel your rib cage expand. **Most people have 12 ribs on each side, but about 1 to 3 percent of people are born with an extra rib.** The extra rib serves no function, and most people aren't bothered by it either. An extra rib can be so thin that it doesn't show up on X-rays and a person might not even know they have it.

Instant Genius

In the human body, there are muscles between the ribs. These muscles help the lungs expand when you breathe.

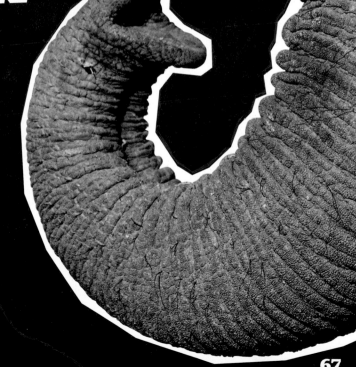

How many muscles does an **elephant's trunk** have?

a. **40**

b. **400**

c. **40,000**

40,000

ELEPHANTS ARE ONE OF THE LARGEST AND STRONGEST LAND ANIMALS ON THE PLANET. **An elephant's trunk has 40,000 muscles and can lift about 700 pounds (318 kg).** The trunk functions both as an arm and a nose to do everything from drinking to grabbing. Elephants also use their trunks to touch and smell each other. These large mammals can also drink up to 2 gallons (8 L) of water at a time and can eat up to 300 pounds (136 kg) of food in a day.

Instant Genius

Some elephants can live up to 70 years.

What were the first modern **bowling balls** made out of?

a. wood and rubber

b. plastic and wood

c. rubber and metal

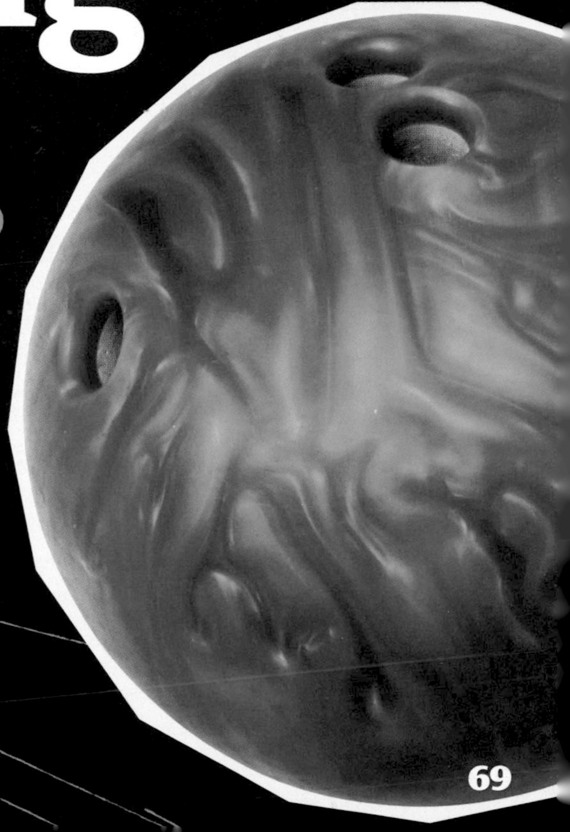

Hannah Diem

ANSWER: a **wood and rubber**

THE FIRST MODERN BOWLING ALLEY WAS BUILT IN 1840 IN NEW YORK CITY. Back then, bowling balls were made of wood and rubber. **Modern bowling balls have three main parts: an inner core, a central core, and an outer layer.** The whole thing is then molded in plastic. Games similar to bowling date back many years. **In fact, archaeologists have found evidence that suggests ancient Egyptians played a sport similar to bowling.**

Instant Genius
The name for three strikes in a row is a "turkey."

70

#32

True or False:

Rainbows sometimes appear at night.

Kohala Coast, Big Island, Hawaii

ANSWER: True

LUNAR RAINBOWS, ALSO CALLED MOONBOWS, ARE RARE OCCURRENCES IN THE NIGHT SKY. **Moonbows are caused when water droplets in the air refract, or bend, the moon's light.** Moonbows are faint compared to rainbows because the moon doesn't give off the same amount of light as the sun does. Because of this, moonbows most often appear white to the human eye. However, moonbow colors have been captured in long-exposure photographs. The conditions need to be just right to create a moonbow. **When a full moon is low in the dark sky and it's raining opposite the moon, you are most likely to catch this rare phenomenon.**

Glacier National Park, Montana

Instant Genius
Double rainbows happen when light bounces twice in a single water droplet.

What's the difference between jam and jelly?

a. They have different ingredients.

b. They are made by different companies.

c. There is no difference.

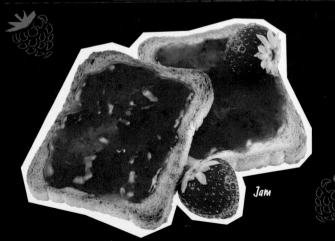

Jam

Jelly

They have different ingredients.

Raspberry Jam

JAM AND JELLY ARE BOTH MADE FROM FRUIT, SUGAR, AND A CARBOHYDRATE CALLED PECTIN THAT IS FOUND IN FRUIT AND MAKES A SUBSTANCE JELL. The difference is that jam is made with crushed fruit and jelly is made with fruit juice. This explains why jam is chunky and jelly is smooth. Jam has a long history. **We don't know exactly when it was invented, but historians think it was first made in the Middle East, possibly around the fourth century.** There is also evidence that the first mention of preserved fruit was in a cookbook that dates back to around the same time. Jam was a common part of the diet in the Middle East, and then the crusaders brought it back to Britain with them. French kings and rulers insisted on having some way to keep their favorite fruit spread from spoiling, which led to the pasteurization of the fruit spread.

NOW YOU KNOW!
The United States produces about 1 billion pounds (450 million kg) of jams, jellies, and fruit spreads a year.

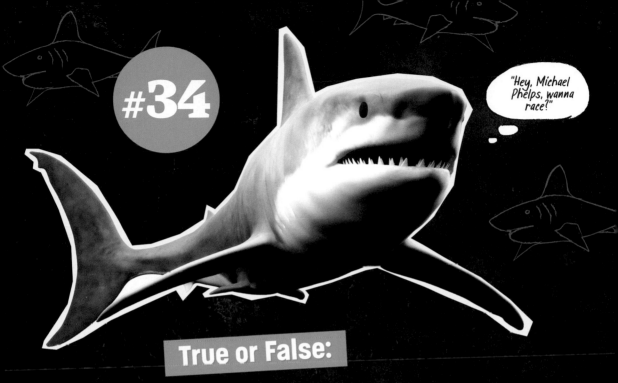

#34

"Hey, Michael Phelps, wanna race?"

True or False:

Great white sharks prefer not to swim long distances.

Instant Genius
Great whites usually travel alone.

ANSWER: False

IN FACT, GREAT WHITES MIGRATE ACROSS THE ENTIRE OCEAN TO GO TO AND FROM THEIR BREEDING GROUNDS. They also migrate to follow their food sources up and down the coasts. Scientists tracked one great white traveling an average of 12,400 miles (20,000 km) in one round-trip migration alone. That's more than two round trips from New York City to Los Angeles! This migration was much longer than scientists had ever seen before for a shark.

NOW YOU KNOW!
An adult great white shark can weigh 5,000 pounds (2,300 kg) on average.

#35

True or False:

Stars
have a life cycle.

An illustration of an exoplanet orbiting two bright stars (seen in the distance)

ANSWER: **True**

JUST LIKE HUMANS, STARS ARE BORN, THEY LIVE THEIR LIVES, AND THEN THEY PASS AWAY. Compared to humans, however, stars live a very long time. **Most stars live from a few million years up to 1 trillion years.** When you are looking at a star, what you are actually seeing is its image from hundreds to millions of years ago. **This is because it takes many light-years for a star's light to come close enough for us to see, and even then the star needs to be in a location where its light can reach our sky.** When you peer up into the night sky at the 9,000 visible stars, you are actually looking at a snapshot of the past.

What is

globophobia?

a. the fear of balloons

c. the fear of clowns

b. the fear of globes

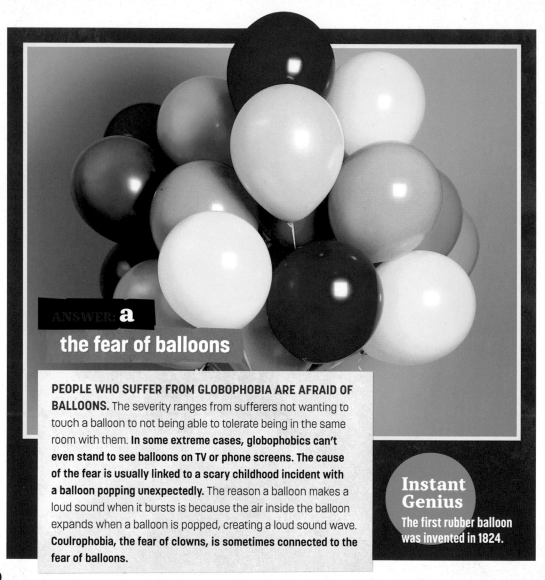

ANSWER: a

the fear of balloons

PEOPLE WHO SUFFER FROM GLOBOPHOBIA ARE AFRAID OF BALLOONS. The severity ranges from sufferers not wanting to touch a balloon to not being able to tolerate being in the same room with them. **In some extreme cases, globophobics can't even stand to see balloons on TV or phone screens. The cause of the fear is usually linked to a scary childhood incident with a balloon popping unexpectedly.** The reason a balloon makes a loud sound when it bursts is because the air inside the balloon expands when a balloon is popped, creating a loud sound wave. **Coulrophobia, the fear of clowns, is sometimes connected to the fear of balloons.**

Instant Genius
The first rubber balloon was invented in 1824.

Where were LEGOS created?

a. Holland

b. Denmark

c. Sweden

lego Masters TV program

ANSWER: b

Denmark

IN 1932, A CARPENTER NAMED OLE KIRK KRISTIANSEN LOST HIS BUSINESS. One day he used a piece of his leftover wood to make a duck for his children. They loved it so much that he was inspired to make toys to sell. Lucky for Lego lovers, these included the early versions of the toy kids love today! **The bricks were named from the first two letters in the words *leg godt,* a phrase that means "play well" in Danish.** Kids have been stacking this super toy ever since. In 1958, a universal system was introduced so that all the bricks in all the sets could fit together. **This means that your Legos can connect with those that belonged to your grandparents!**

The earliest form of **chewing gum** was made from which of these things?

#38

a. seaweed

b. tree sap

c. pollen

83

ANSWER: b — tree sap

THE EARLIEST CHEWING GUM WAS MADE WITH A SUBSTANCE FROM THE SAPODILLA, WHICH IS AN EVERGREEN NATIVE TO THE RAIN FORESTS OF CENTRAL AMERICA AND SOUTHERN MEXICO. Zigzag slashes are cut into the tree's bark, and as the sticky white sap drips, it's collected in little bags. Later, the substance is boiled until it reaches the proper thickness. **The tradition of chewing gum goes as far back as the Aztec and Maya, who chewed this substance, called chicle, when they were hungry and to freshen their breath.** Although natural chicle is still used, most of today's chewing gum contains a human-made substance to make it chewy.

Sapodilla tree

NOW YOU KNOW!
If you ever wondered why bubble gum is pink, the reason is because pink was the only color dye the inventor had left to experiment with. Somehow it stuck!

Instant Genius
Chewing gum burns 11 calories an hour.

Does lightning cause thunder, or does thunder cause lightning?

a. Lightning causes thunder.

b. Thunder causes lightning.

c. It depends on the temperature.

ANSWER: a

Lightning causes thunder.

LIGHTNING IS A SUPER BOLT OF ELECTRICITY THAT'S EVEN HOTTER THAN THE SUN. This electricity cooks the air at a temperature of 50,000° F (27,760° C), which causes the electricity to explode. The hot air vibrates as it moves across the cooler air. **These vibrations bounce off clouds and the ground, and the noise they make is what we call thunder.** Lightning and thunder happen around the same time, but because **light travels about a million times faster than sound, we see it before we hear it.** Thunder can be heard 25 miles (40 km) away.

Instant Genius
Lightning flashes about 40 times a second around the world.

86

Who was the first U.S. president to live in the White House?

#40

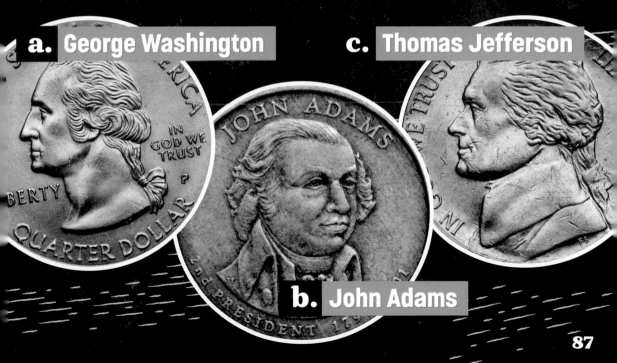

a. George Washington

c. Thomas Jefferson

b. John Adams

Instant Genius

Today, the White House has 132 rooms, a swimming pool, and even a bowling lane.

ANSWER: **b**

John Adams

GEORGE WASHINGTON WAS THE FIRST PRESIDENT OF THE UNITED STATES, BUT HE WAS NOT THE FIRST PRESIDENT TO LIVE IN THE WHITE HOUSE. Though he chose the location of the building in 1791, the construction of the White House didn't start until October 1792, three years into Washington's term (1789–1797). Eight years later, it was ready for the second U.S. president, John Adams, and his wife, Abigail, to move into. Back then, it was called the President's House. President Adams and Mrs. Adams lived in the President's House for only five months, as Adams lost his reelection campaign to Thomas Jefferson.

NOW YOU KNOW!

Enslaved peoples played a major part in the construction of the White House. They were involved with everything from cutting and moving stone to building the walls and roof of the presidential home.

Why are dogs' noses wet?

#41

a. because they dip them in their water bowls

b. because it helps them smell

c. to absorb moisture when they are thirsty

Do I smell treats?

ANSWER: b

because it helps them smell

A DOG'S WET NOSE IS A SIGN OF GOOD HEALTH.
Their noses stay wet because of mucus that is secreted by certain glands located on the tip of the nose. Dogs also keep their noses wet by licking them periodically. Covering the nose in saliva helps keep it clean, which is important because dogs use their noses to explore the world around them. **A dog's nose has 300 million sensory receptors.** When these receptors are kept damp, scent particles are more likely to stick to the nose, allowing a dog to better understand the world.

Instant Genius
Dogs pant to keep themselves cool.

How does a vaccine work?

a. It teaches the immune system how to attack the disease.

b. It seals off the circulation system so that it doesn't come into contact with the disease.

c. It makes you allergic to the disease.

ANSWER: a

It teaches the immune system how to attack the disease.

VACCINES ARE ABLE TO STIMULATE THE IMMUNE SYSTEM AND TEACH IT HOW TO ATTACK CERTAIN DISEASES. Vaccines do this by exposing the immune system to a dead or weakened virus that does not harm the person. This exposure triggers the immune system to respond just like it would if the virus were alive. **The immune system learns how to attack the disease by creating antibodies for the specific disease.** These antibodies have the ability to remember the virus and how to attack it. This means that if the body is exposed to the real virus in the future, the immune system will have already developed the specific antibody to fight the virus before it becomes a problem.

MEASLES

Keep Measles A Memory — Immunize!

For more information, contact:

Instant Genius

Thanks to vaccines, the measles was declared eradicated in the United States in 2000.

#43 How many legs do some **millipedes** have?

a. 40 **b.** 80 **c.** 750

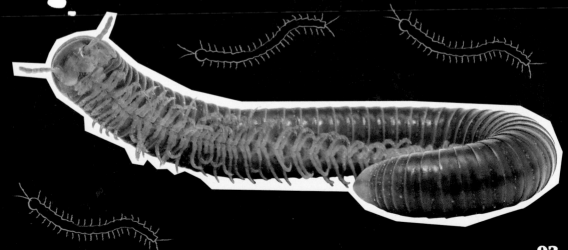

Shoe shopping gets expensive!

ANSWER: C   750

Instant Genius
Centipedes have poisonous claws.

MILLIPEDES ARE KNOWN TO HAVE MANY LEGS, BUT THERE IS ONE SPECIES THAT HAS ALL THE REST BEAT. With 750 legs, *Illacme plenipes* has more legs than any other animal on Earth. This little arthropod is found only in a tiny area of central California, U.S.A., where it lives underground. **It has no eyes, and part of its body is translucent!** And what does it do with all those legs? Well, they help the millipede navigate its environment and grip onto the sandstone rocks found in its habitat.

44

True or False:

A
light-year
measures distance.

Andromeda galaxy

ANSWER: **True**

UNLIKE THE NAME SUGGESTS, A LIGHT-YEAR DOES NOT REFER TO EITHER WATTAGE OR TIME. A light-year is a measurement of the distance light travels in one Earth year. The speed of light is 186,000 miles (300,000 km) a second. This means that in one year, light travels almost 6 trillion miles (10 trillion km). **Scientists use light-years to describe the distance between space objects because distances are so humongous.** If you hopped on board a space shuttle, it would take about 37,200 years to travel one light-year!

Milky Way

Instant Genius

The Milky Way galaxy is about 100,000 light-years across in size.

More people live in the U.S. state of **California** than in the whole country of **Canada.**

#45

New Year's Day, Longtan Park, China

ANSWER: True

Grand Tetons, Wyoming

THE TOTAL POPULATION OF THE STATE OF CALIFORNIA IS ABOUT 39.51 MILLION. This means **California is not only the most populated state in the United States but also home to more people than the entire country of Canada,** which has a population of about 37.94 million. The county of Los Angeles alone has a population of more than 10 million people, making it more populated than many states and even than numerous countries around the world.

Instant Genius
Wyoming is the least populated state in the United States with about 579,000 residents.

Which
animal has
Jane Goodall
spent her life studying?

#46

c. the sloth

a. the chimpanzee

b. the lion

Instant Genius

Through her observation of chimpanzees, Jane Goodall discovered that chimps use tools.

ANSWER: a

the chimpanzee

JANE GOODALL IS KNOWN FOR HER PIONEERING WORK AS A PRIMATOLOGIST, A SCIENTIST WHO STUDIES PRIMATES SUCH AS CHIMPANZEES, GORILLAS, AND ORANGUTANS. Her focus was on chimps, and she took a unique approach to learning about these animals: She lived among them. In 1960, at the age of 26, Goodall traveled to Gombe Forest in the African country of Tanzania. She chose to research chimpanzees because little was known about them at the time. She slowly integrated herself into the chimpanzee community, where she could observe the animals closely. She learned a great deal about how chimps live and communicate and she shared her discoveries with the world. Goodall still works to educate people about chimpanzees and the importance of protecting them and their natural environment.

True or False:

There are spelling mistakes engraved on the

Stanley Cup.

#47

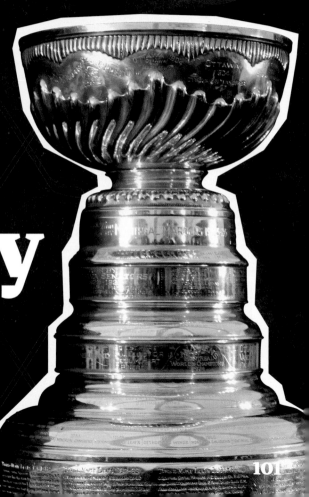

101

KEAN MCINNE A PRONOVOST ...
H RICHARD J GUY TALBOT ROBERT TURNER   JEAN GUY TALBOT HECTOR D
H HECTOR DUBOIS LARRY AUBUT TRAINER S   LARRY AUBUT TRAINER

"Bqstqn" Bruins misspelled

BOSTON BRUINS 1971-72   CLUB DE HOCKEY

WESTON W. ADAMS CHAIRMAN OF BOARD   JACQUES COURTOIS PRE
WESTON W. ADAMS JR. PRESIDENT   PETER BRONFMAN CHAIR
SHELEY DAVIS VICE PRESIDENT   EDWARD BRONFMAN EX. V
CHARLES W. MULCAHY JR. VICE PRES. GEN. COUNSEL   HENRI RICHARD JACQUES
F.H. J. PETERS V. PRES. TREAS. MILT SCHMIDT G. MAN.   YVAN COURNOYER JACQ
TOM JOHNSON COACH BOBBY ORR GERRY CHEEVERS   SERGE SAVARD PETER
ED JOHNSTON DALLAS SMITH DEREK SANDERSON   REJEAN HOULE CLAUD
CAROL VADNAIS PHIL ESPOSITO FRED STANFIELD   FRANK MAHOVLICH J.
DON AWREY TED GREEN KEN HODGE JOHN BUCYK   GUY LAFLEUR ROBER
WAYNE CASHMAN JOHN MCKENZIE ED WESTFALL   MURRY WILSON LAR
MIKE WALTON GARNET BAILEY DON MARCOTTE   ROBERT WILLIAMS
DAN CANNEY TRAINER JOHN FORRISTALL ASS. TRAC.   EDDY PALCHAK

ANSWER: True

FIRST GIVEN IN 1894, THE STANLEY CUP IS THE OLDEST TROPHY TO BE AWARDED IN PROFESSIONAL SPORTS IN NORTH AMERICA. Unlike other sports, instead of minting a new trophy each year, the original one is reused and updated with the names of the winning team's members engraved on it. Not that they always get it perfectly right! **There are permanent spelling mistakes engraved on the Stanley Cup.** For example, the name of the 1980–81 New York Islanders is misspelled as "Ilanders," and the 1971–72 Boston Bruins name is misspelled as "Bqstqn Bruins." **Engraving names on the cup became a tradition in 1924, and there are now more than 2,000 names displayed.**

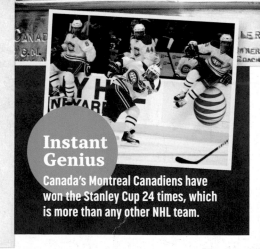

Instant Genius
Canada's Montreal Canadiens have won the Stanley Cup 24 times, which is more than any other NHL team.

What color blood do **horseshoe** crabs have?

#48

a. blue

b. red

c. They don't have blood.

103

NOW YOU KNOW!
Researchers use horseshoe crab blood to test drugs and vaccines to make sure that they are free of harmful bacteria.

ANSWER: a blue

HORSESHOE CRABS HAVE BLUE BLOOD BECAUSE OF THE AMOUNT OF COPPER THEIR BLOOD CONTAINS. **When copper mixes with oxygen, it causes a blue color. There are four different species of horseshoe crabs. One species is found up and down the east coast of North America and three others in the Indian and Pacific Oceans.** Horseshoe crabs crush up their food, which includes worms, clams, and algae, with their 10 legs to get it into bite-size pieces before they eat. **Female horseshoe crabs can be as big as 18 inches (46 cm),** which is about the size of an extra-large pizza. **Males only grow to be about 15 inches (38 cm).**

Instant Genius
Horseshoe crabs have nine eyes.

You grow an entirely new surface to your **skin** every four weeks.

#49

Close up view of the surface of the skin

ANSWER: **True**

THE SKIN IS THE BODY'S LARGEST ORGAN. It acts as a waterproof barrier to keep out harmful toxins and the sun's ultraviolet light. The outer layer is called the epidermis and it's constantly renewing itself. **Your skin is the thickest on your feet and the thinnest on your eyelids.** Each month, the surface cells are replaced by new ones growing beneath them. **With 350,000 dead skin cells shed every minute, the** average person releases about half their bodyweight of skin cells over the course of a lifetime.

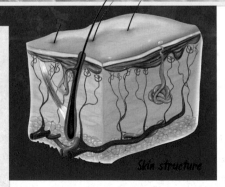

Skin structure

#50

Who would win in a **smelling contest?**

a. a dog   b. a salmon   c. It would be a tie.

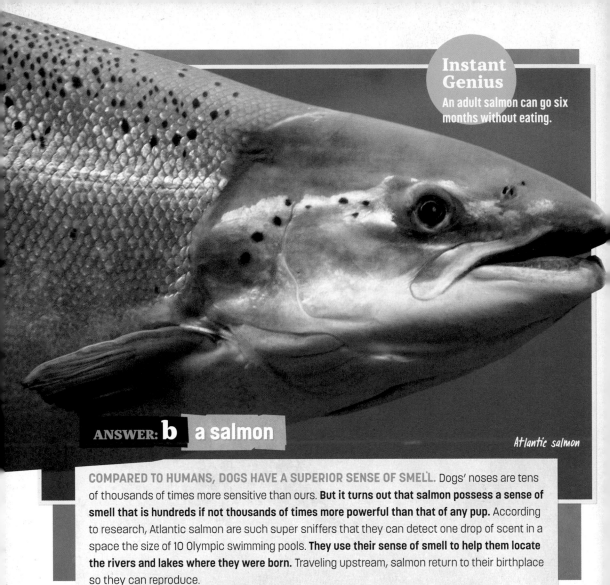

ANSWER: b a salmon

Atlantic salmon

COMPARED TO HUMANS, DOGS HAVE A SUPERIOR SENSE OF SMELL. Dogs' noses are tens of thousands of times more sensitive than ours. **But it turns out that salmon possess a sense of smell that is hundreds if not thousands of times more powerful than that of any pup.** According to research, Atlantic salmon are such super sniffers that they can detect one drop of scent in a space the size of 10 Olympic swimming pools. **They use their sense of smell to help them locate the rivers and lakes where they were born.** Traveling upstream, salmon return to their birthplace so they can reproduce.

When did **trick-or-treating** become widely popular in America?

a. in the 18th century

b. right before the first Thanksgiving in 1621

c. during the 1930s

#51

Trick or treat!

ANSWER: C

during the 1930s

NOW YOU KNOW!
One of the earliest uses of the phrase "trick or treat" in pop culture was in a *Peanuts* comic strip in 1951. The following year, Disney produced a Donald Duck cartoon called *Trick or Treat*.

COMMUNITIES STARTED ORGANIZING THE FAMILY-FRIENDLY TRADITION OF TRICK-OR-TREATING IN THE 1930S. Then, during World War II (1939–1945), sugar was rationed, which meant fewer treats to give out, and the tradition stalled. **Once the war was over, trick-or-treating resumed and soon became a popular pastime on October 31.** And since a lack of sugar was no longer a problem, candy companies seized the opportunity to sell sweets by advertising their candies. **Today, Americans spend more than $2.5 billion on Halloween candy each year.**

PEANUTS

USA 34

Which is the
hottest
planet
in the solar
system?

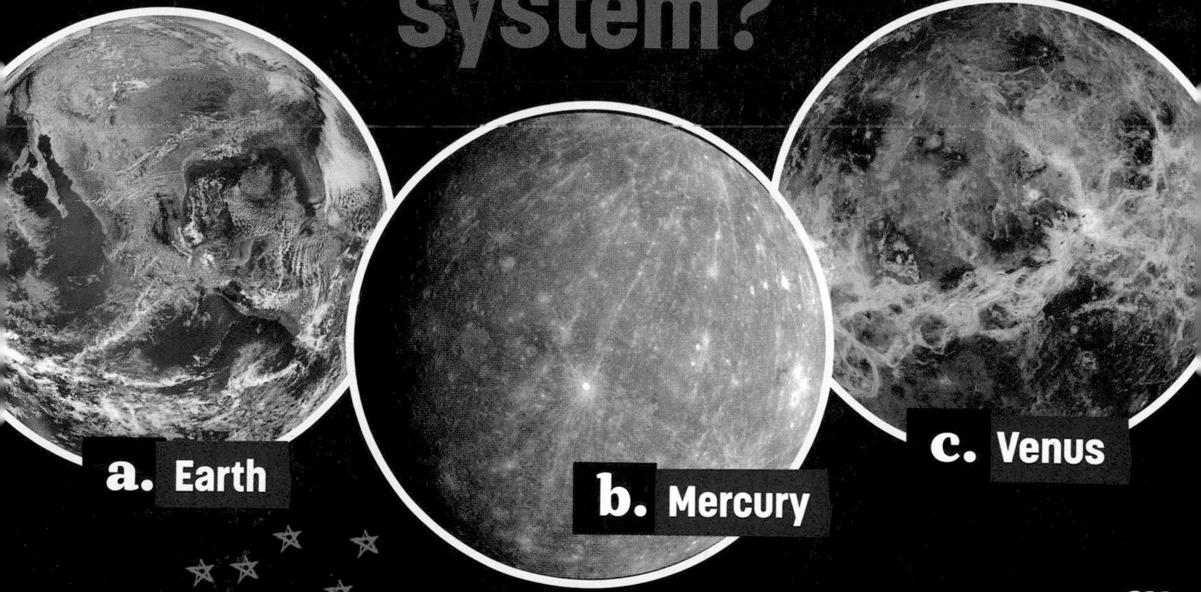

a. Earth

b. Mercury

c. Venus

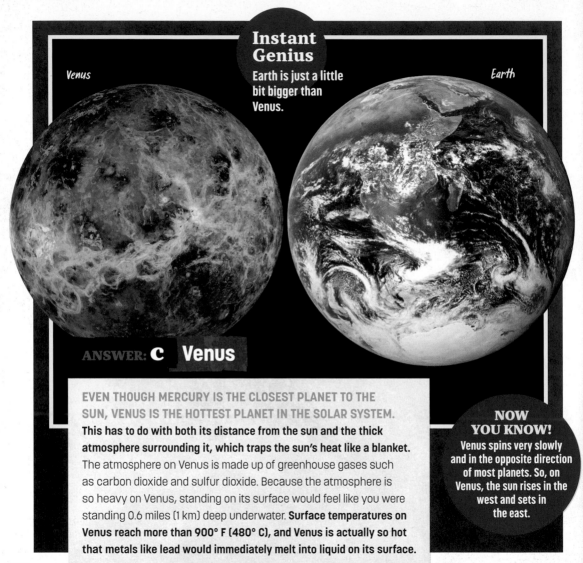

Venus

Earth

ANSWER: **c** **Venus**

EVEN THOUGH MERCURY IS THE CLOSEST PLANET TO THE SUN, VENUS IS THE HOTTEST PLANET IN THE SOLAR SYSTEM. This has to do with both its distance from the sun and the thick atmosphere surrounding it, which traps the sun's heat like a blanket. The atmosphere on Venus is made up of greenhouse gases such as carbon dioxide and sulfur dioxide. Because the atmosphere is so heavy on Venus, standing on its surface would feel like you were standing 0.6 miles (1 km) deep underwater. **Surface temperatures on Venus reach more than 900° F (480° C), and Venus is actually so hot that metals like lead would immediately melt into liquid on its surface.**

NOW YOU KNOW!
Venus spins very slowly and in the opposite direction of most planets. So, on Venus, the sun rises in the west and sets in the east.

True or False:

Like domestic cats, **big cats** hate getting wet.

#53

I forgot my umbrella.

ANSWER: False

RESEARCHERS THINK MOST DOMESTIC CATS EVOLVED IN DRY AREAS WHERE THERE WASN'T MUCH WATER AROUND. Since domestic cats are generally unaccustomed to being in or around water, a wet coat can be heavy and make a cat feel cold and uncomfortable. Water on a cat's fur can also result in the fur becoming ruffled. Many wild cats, however, are different. Cats that live in warmer climates, such as tigers, leopards, jaguars, and lions, can often be found lounging in watering holes and lakes. The water keeps them cool under the hot sun. Wild cats also teach their cubs to play in water.

True or False:

When it is summer in the United States, it is winter in Australia.

#54

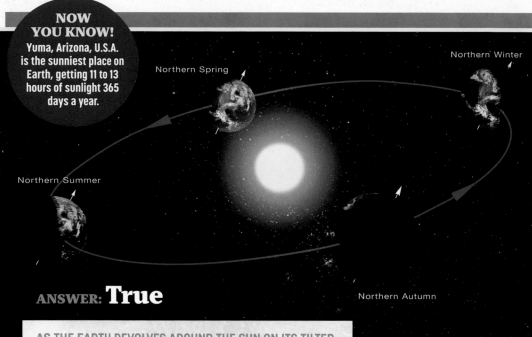

Northern Spring

Northern Winter

Northern Summer

Northern Autumn

ANSWER: True

AS THE EARTH REVOLVES AROUND THE SUN ON ITS TILTED AXIS, WE EXPERIENCE SEASONS. **The four seasons—spring, summer, fall, and winter—follow a cycle.** Each season has its own average temperature, general weather, and amount of sunlight depending on how far a place is from Earth's equator. **In the Northern Hemisphere, the winter solstice begins on December 21 or 22, which has the shortest day and longest night of the year. The summer solstice begins on June 21 or 22, when the Northern Hemisphere experiences the longest day and the shortest night of the year.** Because of the way the planet rotates on its axis, the seasons in the Northern Hemisphere, where the United States is, are the opposite of the Southern Hemisphere, where Australia is located. **This makes our seasons opposites.**

Instant Genius

Abisko, Sweden; Svalbard, Norway; Fairbanks, Alaska; and Inuvik, Canada, are some of the places that experience darkness all winter and sunlight all summer.

Where was **basketball** invented?

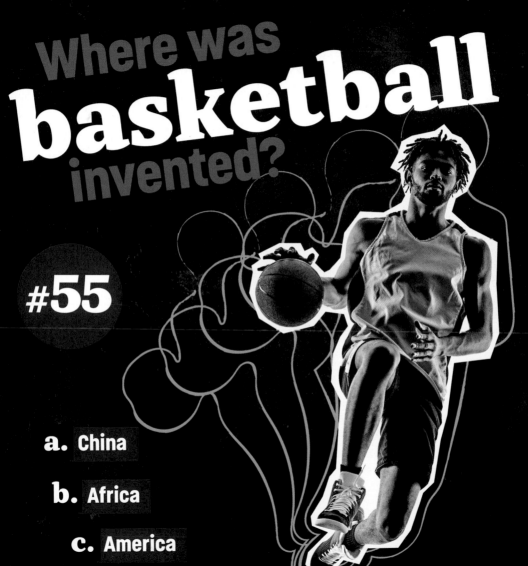

#55

a. China

b. Africa

c. America

ANSWER: **C** **America**

IN 1891, A TEACHER IN SPRINGFIELD, MASSACHUSETTS, WAS TRYING TO FIGURE OUT A WAY TO KEEP HIS GYM CLASS OCCUPIED DURING WINTRY DAYS. The teacher had the idea to use two boxes (he ended up using peach baskets) nailed to two balcony rails as goals where a ball could be dropped. Then he quickly invented some rules for the game, and the rest is history. Much has changed since that first gym class. **The ball used by the students in Springfield was modeled after the soccer ball with outside stitching, which made dribbling difficult.** Eventually, the lace-free ball was constructed for better bouncing.

The human body produces millions of

blood cells

per second.

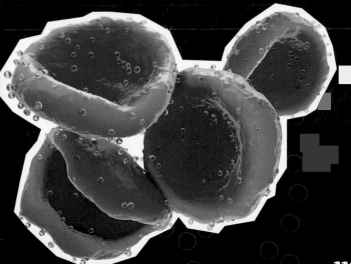

Red blood cells

ANSWER: **True**

EACH ONE OF US PRODUCES ABOUT 2 MILLION BLOOD CELLS PER SECOND. Millions of blood cells naturally die every second. Our bodies keep replacing them in order for us to survive. Stem cells, located in our bone marrow, produce blood cells. If the body is ever running low on blood cells, special cells in the kidneys will release a hormone into the bloodstream that will reach the bone marrow and signal that blood cell production needs to increase.

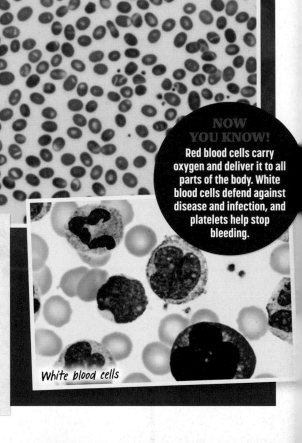

White blood cells

How much water does a
mile (1.6 km)
of fog hold?

a. none

b. 50 gallons (189 L)

c. 56,000 gallons (211,983 L)

Carpathian Mountains, Ukraine

ANSWER: C   56,000 gallons (211,983 L)

FOG IS A VISIBLE CLOUD FILLED WITH TINY WATER DROPLETS OR ICE CRYSTALS THAT HANGS NEAR EARTH'S SURFACE. When warm air chills, it turns to fog because cold air contains less vapor than warm air. **Fog usually disappears with daylight because the sun warms up the air, which evaporates the water vapor.** Fog is often found near large bodies of water and in valleys near mountains. **Fog is more likely to appear at dawn or at night, when temperatures are lower than they are during the day.**

Koala bears
aren't really bears.

#58

ANSWER: True

KOALAS ARE A PART OF A GROUP OF MAMMALS KNOWN AS MARSUPIALS, ANIMALS THAT HAVE POUCHES ON THEIR BELLIES WHERE THEY CAN HOLD THEIR YOUNG. **Koalas are related to kangaroos and opossums and are only found in the forests of Australia.** They grow to be about 2.5 feet (76 cm) tall on average. Real bears, on the other hand, are mammals that are related to racoons and dogs. **They are found in North and South America, Asia, and Europe, and bears are much larger than koalas.** In fact, polar bears, which are considered the largest of the eight bear species, can grow to be 10 feet (3 m) tall and weigh up to 1,500 pounds (680 kg)!

NOW YOU KNOW!

Eucalyptus leaves are a koala's main diet, and a koala can pack away about 2 pounds (1 kg) of leaves in just one day.

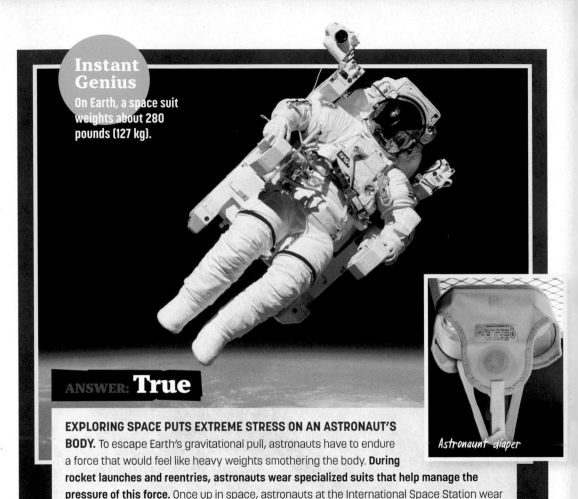

Instant Genius

On Earth, a space suit weights about 280 pounds (127 kg).

ANSWER: **True**

Astronaunt diaper

EXPLORING SPACE PUTS EXTREME STRESS ON AN ASTRONAUT'S BODY. To escape Earth's gravitational pull, astronauts have to endure a force that would feel like heavy weights smothering the body. **During rocket launches and reentries, astronauts wear specialized suits that help manage the pressure of this force.** Once up in space, astronauts at the International Space Station wear different space suits that are highly pressurized and temperature controlled when they head outside for space walks. **When they are out in space, they can't take off their space suits to go to the bathroom, so scientists designed the Maximum Absorbency Garment, or MAG, which is a kind of super diaper, so they can relieve themselves without worry.** Astronauts also wear MAGs during liftoff, reentry, and landing.

Only the government was allowed to use early computers.

#60

Scientists at the National Physical Laboratory in Teddington, England working to develop an early computer in the 1950s known as Pilot ACE.

ANSWER: True

EARLY COMPUTERS WERE FIRST CREATED AS A COMMUNICATIONS SYSTEM BACK IN THE 1950S TO USE AGAINST THE SOVIET UNION DURING THE COLD WAR, BUT IT WASN'T AVAILABLE TO THE PUBLIC. **For this reason, computers were government-owned.** No one besides certain scientists, military personnel, and university staff were authorized to use them. They were also being used to plan for nuclear attacks and spy missions. **These supercomputers were extremely heavy, some even weighing as much as 30 tons (27 metric t).**

The ORDVAC was an early computer built by the University of Illinois, U.S.A., starting in 1949.

Where was the first permanent **English settlement** in North America?

a. Boston, Massachusetts

b. Washington, D.C.

c. Jamestown, Virginia

Instant Genius

Native Americans had been living in the area that is now Virginia for more than 12,000 years before the arrival of the English.

NOW YOU KNOW!

The colonialization of the Americas had a huge impact on Indigenous peoples. Their lands and food sources were being destroyed and diseases brought by the Europeans killed many people. They were struggling to preserve their way of life.

ANSWER: C

Jamestown, Virginia

IN 1606, THREE SHIPS SET SAIL FROM ENGLAND TO NORTH AMERICA CARRYING 104 ENGLISH MEN AND BOYS. The following year, the new settlers chose what is now Jamestown, Virginia, U.S.A., to settle because of its location. **Jamestown was surrounded by water on three sides, making it easy to defend against possible invaders.** It also offered a harbor with water deep enough for the ships to dock. **Unfortunately, famine and disease from unhealthy drinking water killed many of the original settlers.** If it wasn't for gifts of food from the local Powhatan Native Americans, none of the settlers would have survived. But the relationship between the Powhatan and the English became difficult because of the growing demands of the English. Fighting then began between the Powhatan and settlers. The harsh winter of 1609-1610 nearly killed the remaining original settlers. **More English arrived in an effort to help. In 1612, the cash crop of tobacco was introduced and money made from selling it helped the settlement survive.**

What percentage of all animals are insects?

a. **25 percent**

b. **50 percent**

c. **80 percent**

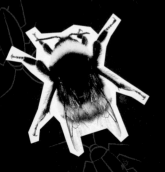

ANSWER: C

80 percent

NOW
YOU KNOW!
Ants are the most numerous
insects in the world. With
more than 10,000 ant species,
there are from 10 trillion to
100,000 trillion individual
ants on Earth.

THERE ARE MORE THAN 900,000 KNOWN LIVING INSECT SPECIES, AND MANY MORE THAT HAVE NOT YET BEEN NAMED BY SCIENTISTS. **Some researchers think the real number could be as high as 30 million!** Beetles represent the largest percentage, making up a third of all known insect species. Not only are there many different varieties of insects on Earth, but they also take up the most biomass, or room, on our planet. **Right now, there are 10 quintillion (10,000,000,000,000,000,000) insects alive. That's about 1.25 billion insects for each human on the planet.**

The longest-ruling leader of *Russia* was a woman.

#63

Catherine the Great

SOPHIE FRIEDERIKE AUGUSTE ANHALT-ZERBST, BETTER KNOWN AS CATHERINE THE GREAT, WAS THE LONGEST-RULING FEMALE LEADER OF RUSSIA, EVEN THOUGH SHE WASN'T RUSSIAN. Her father was a German prince and she grew up in the country that is now Poland. When she married a Russian prince, she took the name Catherine. **She came to power in 1762 following an uprising that overthrew her husband, who was an unpopular king.** She took the opportunity to rule the country herself and led the Russian Empire for 34 years. **Catherine was known as a skilled military leader, conquering new territories to grow her empire.**

Russian coin

How many **sweat glands** are in each of your feet?

#64

a. 20,000

b. 100,000   c. 125,000

Pee-yew!

ANSWER: C

125,000

NOW YOU KNOW!

Eating spicy foods can cause sweating because a chemical in the food, called capsaicin, makes your brain think your body temperature is going up.

Spicy eggplant and tomatoes

FEET CAN GET REALLY SWEATY! Each foot has about 125,000 sweat glands that function as built-in air conditioners that can produce half a pint (0.25 L) of liquid daily. Eww! Overall, the human body has between 2 and 4 million sweat glands, with the highest density on the soles on the feet and palms of the hand. **Sweat is made up mostly of water, and it's actually odorless.** The reason we sometimes smell when we sweat is because bacteria on our bodies break down sweat, and that's what causes the stink.

The first clock was a *sundial.*

Forbidden City, China

ANSWER: True

SUNDIALS WERE USED THROUGHOUT ANCIENT HUMAN HISTORY AS ONE OF THE EARLIEST TOOLS FOR TIMEKEEPING. Sundials are used by placing a straight object, like a stick, upright out of the ground and then drawing a circle around it. Marks are made along the outside of the circle for each hour. Sundials are easiest to read when it's sunny outside. **The shadow that's created by the stick tracks the time of day as the sun rises and sets. When the sun is at its highest around noon, there will be almost no shadow.** As the day continues, the shadow moves around the circle similarly to how hands move on a clock.

Why didn't people **smile** in old photos?

a. **because they were hungry**

b. **to hide their teeth**

c. **because smiling wasn't considered polite**

ANSWER: C **because smiling wasn't considered polite**

BEFORE PHOTOGRAPHY CAME ALONG IN THE 1820S, IT WAS COMMON FOR PEOPLE TO HAVE THEIR PORTRAITS PAINTED, AND AT THAT TIME SMILING WAS THOUGHT INAPPROPRIATE. It's possible that when people were photographed, they were taking their cues for posing from painted portraits. **In fact, when people smiled broadly, they were often thought of as strange.** A closed-mouth smile started to become more common in the 1920s and 1930s.

Instant Genius
Photographers started asking people to say "Cheese!" around the 1940s.

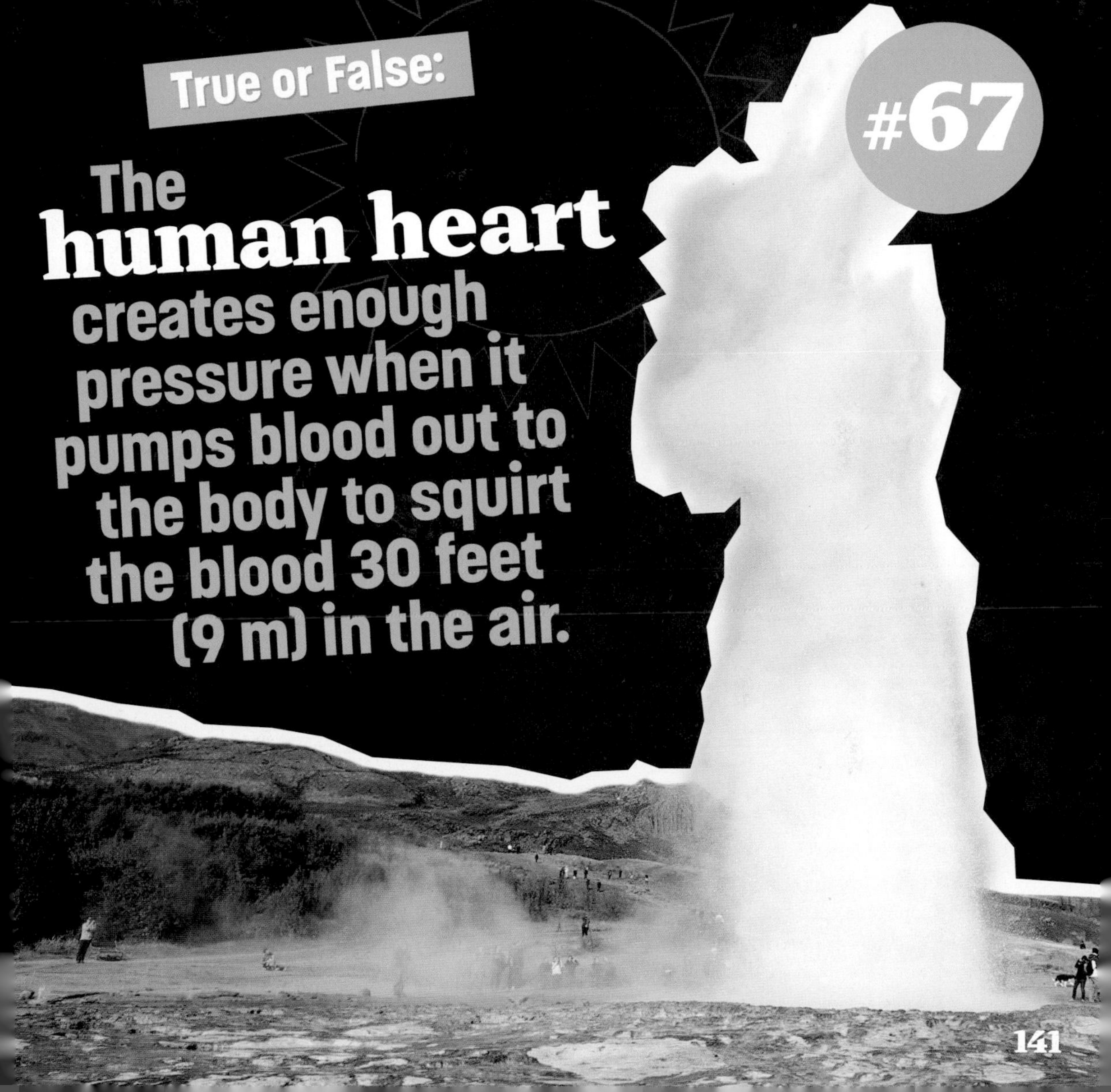

#67

The
human heart
creates enough
pressure when it
pumps blood out to
the body to squirt
the blood 30 feet
(9 m) in the air.

141

NOW YOU KNOW!
Many of the muscles in the body get tired after being used a lot, for example after a long walk or run. But your heart doesn't get tired of beating.

ANSWER: True

EVERY VITAL ORGAN AND TISSUE IN OUR BODIES NEEDS A CONSTANT SUPPLY OF OXYGEN TO SURVIVE, AND IT IS THE PRIMARY JOB OF THE HEART TO DELIVER IT TO THEM. The heart needs to have an incredibly strong beat for it to continuously pump blood to the lungs so that the blood can be oxygenated and then distributed all over the body. **The heart's beating has so much power that it has the ability to squirt blood 30 feet (9 m). In order to keep it pumping at a steady rate, the heart has its own electrical system.** Special cells start the heartbeat by sending out signals to the heart that tell it to pump. **These signals are sent out regularly, keeping the heart pumping at a constant rate.**

Instant Genius
The human heart can pump up to 7 gallons (26 L) of blood a minute.

#68

Why do female tarantulas eat the male after mating?

a. because they're hungry

b. because the male would kill them

c. to protect the babies

Tarantula eating her mate

ANSWER: a **because they're hungry**

SPIDER CANNIBALISM IS WHEN A SPIDER EATS ONE OF ITS OWN KIND. **In many different spider species, including tarantulas, the female will often kill and eat the male after mating.** If the male is smaller than the female, she will take the opportunity to eat her mate if she's hungry. When the male is larger, she'll leave him alone and feed on the usual diet of grasshoppers and crickets. No wonder there's such a difference between how long males and females live: **Male tarantulas live for 7 to 8 years, while females can live 20 to 25 years.**

True or False:

Astronauts are not able to use a
ballpoint pen
in space.

#69

145

ANSWER: **True**

Pilot Gordon Fullerton

A REGULAR PEN DOESN'T WRITE IN SPACE. This is because the ink needs gravity to move down inside the pen to the ball at the tip. In space, there is no gravity. Pencils do write in space, and NASA astronauts did use them during the first missions in the 1960s, but they soon switched to special space pens, because pencils posed a hazard. How? When the tips of the lead broke off, they floated around in the air without gravity to make them fall. **At about the time the Apollo missions were happening in the 1960s, a man named Paul Fisher created ballpoint pens that would work in space. Instead of relying on gravity to make them work, these pens had an ink cartridge that used pressure to make the ink come out.** In 1967, NASA bought these specialty pens for the Apollo astronauts. Today, astronauts still use these pens!

More than 75 percent of the **world's diet** is produced from 12 plant and 5 animal species.

ANSWER: True

$2 LB.

MORE THAN 75 PERCENT OF THE WORLD'S DIET IS PRODUCED FROM 12 PLANT AND 5 ANIMAL SPECIES. **Wheat, corn, and rice make up 60 percent of the plant-based calories in our food. The top animal species, if you eat meat, include chicken, cattle, and pigs.** According to experts, our limited diet is not good for our planet. This is because global farming can lead to habitat destruction, which leads to the destruction of our environment. Overfarming can also deplete the soil of nutrients. **Studies show that eating more plant-based foods, like beans and veggies, and less meat, can be good for human health and for the planet.**

The brain
does not feel pain.

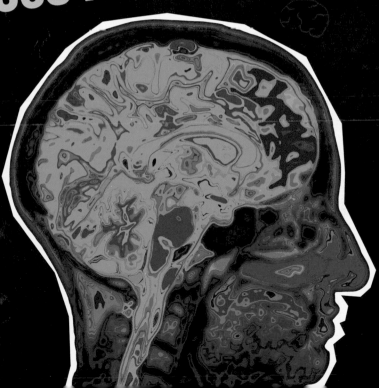

71

149

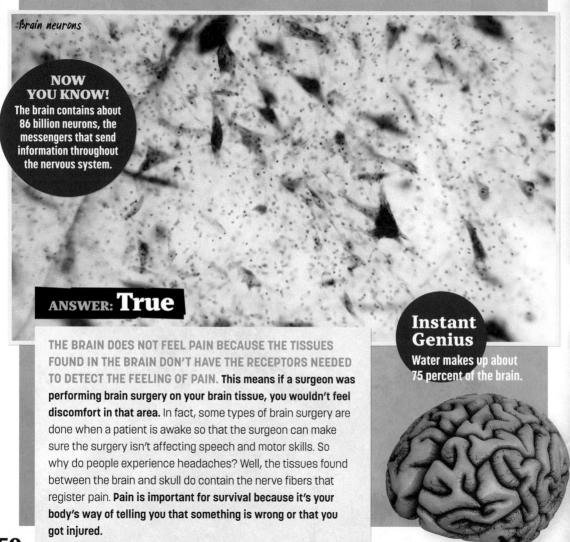

Brain neurons

NOW YOU KNOW!
The brain contains about 86 billion neurons, the messengers that send information throughout the nervous system.

ANSWER: True

Instant Genius
Water makes up about 75 percent of the brain.

THE BRAIN DOES NOT FEEL PAIN BECAUSE THE TISSUES FOUND IN THE BRAIN DON'T HAVE THE RECEPTORS NEEDED TO DETECT THE FEELING OF PAIN. **This means if a surgeon was performing brain surgery on your brain tissue, you wouldn't feel discomfort in that area.** In fact, some types of brain surgery are done when a patient is awake so that the surgeon can make sure the surgery isn't affecting speech and motor skills. So why do people experience headaches? Well, the tissues found between the brain and skull do contain the nerve fibers that register pain. **Pain is important for survival because it's your body's way of telling you that something is wrong or that you got injured.**

What is Dr. Martin Luther King, Jr., known for?

a. ending the Vietnam War

c. serving as one of the leaders of the civil rights movement

b. setting an Olympic record

Martin Luther King, Jr., at the March on Washington, in Washington, D.C.

ANSWER: C serving as one of the leaders of the civil rights movement

IN THE 1960S, NOT EVERYONE HAD EQUAL RIGHTS IN AMERICA. Back then, Black people were segregated from White people. This meant that Black people had to use separate entrances, bathrooms, and water fountains. They were not even allowed to sit at the front of a bus simply because of the color of their skin. Black children also had to go to different schools. Dr. Martin Luther King, Jr., was a Baptist minister who inspired and led both Black and White people who disagreed with the racist segregation policy to push for segregation laws to be changed. **He was famous for believing in and promoting nonviolent protests such as sit-ins and marches. In his legendary "I Have a Dream" speech at the March on Washington in 1963, Dr. King encouraged people to envision a better world where everyone was treated fairly.** Due to Dr. King's efforts, and those of many other civil rights leaders and activists who worked alongside him, the Civil Rights Act of 1964 was passed, making segregation in public places illegal. **The struggle for equality continues today, but Dr. King's contribution to the cause set America on a path to becoming a more just and equitable country. His work also inspired many people around the world to fight for equal rights.**

Penguins

are the only birds that can't fly.

let's just wing it.

73

Penguin toboggan, Antarctica

NOW YOU KNOW!

Not all penguin species live in Antarctica. Some are found in parts of Australia, New Zealand, South America, and Africa.

ANSWER: False

EVEN THOUGH PENGUINS HAVE WINGS, THEY ACT MORE LIKE FLIPPERS THAT ARE USED TO SWIFTLY PROPEL THE PENGUINS THROUGH THE WATER. Of all penguin species, gentoos are known to be the fastest swimmers. They can reach speeds of up to 22 miles an hour (35 kmh) in the water. In addition to swimming, penguins that live in icy environments are known to lie down on their bellies and glide on the ice in an act known as tobogganing. **Penguins are not the only birds that can't fly, though. Kiwis, kakapos, cassowaries, emus, ostriches, and a number of other species can't fly either.** Most species of flightless birds live in New Zealand.

Instant Genius

Penguins have a thick layer of blubber under their skin to keep them warm.

What allows a **thermos** to keep drinks hot and cold?

#74

a. water

b. a type of plastic

c. the absence of air

Dewar or vacuum flask diagram

cup

cork stopper

vacuum

silvered surface

double walled - metal or plastic container

hot or cold liquid

insulated support

the absence of air

THE THERMOS WAS INVENTED IN 1892 BY A SCOTTISH SCIENTIST. A thermos is a bottle made out of metal or plastic that has two walls inside of it. When the thermos is made, the air between the two walls is sucked out, which creates a vacuum. A vacuum is a place where nothing exists. **The vacuum serves as insulation to keep liquids at the same temperature as when they are poured inside.** The thermos's hollow walls prevent the heat from escaping, keeping your hot chocolate hot. **The double walls also keep cool air from escaping, keeping your lemonade chilled.**

Instant Genius

Hot drinks such as coffee are often served between 160° F (71° C) and 185° F (85° C).

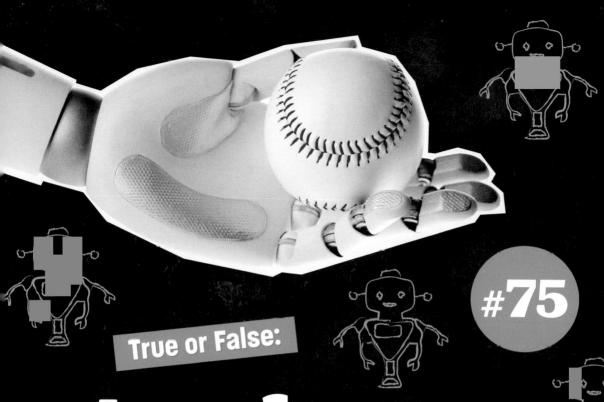

True or False:

A robot
can find and grab an object
that is hidden from view.

#75

Mars rover

ANSWER: **True**

SCIENTISTS HAVE BEEN HARD AT WORK FIGURING OUT HOW TO CREATE ROBOTS WITH SUPERHUMAN SENSIBILITIES.
Artificial intelligence, called AI for short, has given robots the capability to see and touch. Researchers at the Massachusetts Institute of Technology (MIT) developed a technology that gives a robot the ability to complete a task that can even be difficult for humans to do—locating and grabbing objects that are hidden from view. **This new robot called "RF-Grasp" uses radio waves and computer vision to sense and pinpoint objects that are behind walls.**

Hydraulic mechanic arm packing cartons

#76

A popular New Year's tradition in Greece is **smashing pomegranates.**

Oliebollen, a traditional Dutch pastry

ANSWER: **True**

DEPENDING ON WHERE YOU ARE IN THE WORLD, THERE ARE MANY WAYS TO CELEBRATE THE NEW YEAR. In Greece, people hang onions on their doors to symbolize rebirth and smash pomegranates against their doors for good luck. In Japan, people slurp soba noodles to gain strength. In Brazil, white flowers and candles are tossed into the sea and white clothing is worn as a symbol of peace and for good luck. In Spain, people eat exactly 12 grapes at the stroke of midnight. Each grape represents one month of the year, and the tradition is considered to bring good luck. And in the Netherlands, where New Year's temperatures are frigid, the Dutch eat warm, sweet deep-fried dough called *oliebollen*.

Japanese soba noodles

#77

How old is the
solar system?

a. less than 5,000 years old

b. almost 1 million years old

c. more than 4 billion years old

Our universe is estimated to be about 13.8 billion years old.

ANSWER: C

more than 4 billion years old

OUR SOLAR SYSTEM IS SOME 4.5 BILLION YEARS OLD. Scientists know this from studying meteorites found on Earth. **Scientists compared meteorites that were almost 5 billion years old, and then compared them with the oldest rocks found on Earth, which dated back to 3.8 billion years ago.** In these rocks there were chemical fossils that showed signs of microscopic life occurring all the way back then. **Scientists think that the solar system formed 4.5 billion years ago out of a cloud of gas and dust.** This gas and dust formed a cloud called a solar nebula. The gravity at the center of the solar nebula formed the sun. **The sun's gravity then took in 99 percent of the matter. Then the leftover material grouped together to make all of the moons, planets, and asteroids.**

How many nights do people of the Jewish faith celebrate Hanukkah?

a. seven nights **b.** eight nights **c.** nine nights

Instant Genius
The menorah is always lit from left to right.

ANSWER: **b** **eight nights**

HANUKKAH IS THE FESTIVAL OF LIGHTS IN JEWISH CULTURE. Because Jewish holidays are based on the lunar calendar, the dates change year to year, but the holiday usually occurs in December. Friends and family come together to reaffirm their faith and eat delicious foods that are rooted in Jewish tradition. **These eight nights of celebration are held to remember the story of how the Second Temple of Jerusalem survived an intense conflict, with only one small jar of holy oil remaining to light the sacred lamp.** As the story goes, there was enough oil in the jar to last one night. However, the lamp remained lit for eight days and nights. This is why the festival lasts for eight days and the menorah is lit on each of those days.

Which insect inflicts the

most painful bite?

a. the scorpion

b. the conga ant

c. the black widow spider

conga ant

NOW YOU KNOW!

Conga ants like to prey on the glasswing butterfly. To protect itself, this butterfly has evolved to produce a chemical that tastes icky to conga ants so they will leave it alone.

ANSWER: b

the conga ant

AN ENTOMOLOGIST (A SCIENTIST WHO STUDIES INSECTS) CREATED A SCALE THAT GOES FROM ONE TO FOUR TO RATE THE PAIN LEVEL OF AN INSECT STING BASED ON THE STRENGTH OF EACH INSECT'S VENOM. **Topping the chart with the most painful sting is the tiny conga ant, also known as the bullet ant.** While these ants are not usually aggressive, they will attack to defend their nest, and their sting has been described as "burning" and "excruciating." **The conga ant's paralyzing toxin, which is not lethal to humans, is being studied as a possible medicine.**

Warrior Wasp

Instant Genius

The only other insects capable of producing chart-topping pain are tarantula hawks and warrior wasps.

Which area of the world is home to the most people with red hair?

a. the United Kingdom and Ireland

b. the United States

c. Scandinavia

NOW YOU KNOW!
In the Middle Ages, people with green eyes and red hair were suspected of being vampires, werewolves, and witches.

ANSWER: a

the United Kingdom and Ireland

COMPARED TO OTHER HAIR COLORS, RED IS CONSIDERED RARE. Only about 1 to 2 percent of people around the world have it. In Ireland and Scotland, however, the percentages are higher, with about 10 percent of Irish and 6 percent of Scottish people having red hair. We inherit hair color from our parents. According to new research, eight genes are associated with being a redhead. In Ireland and Scotland, more people carry red-hair genes, even if they don't have red hair themselves. **Many redheads have very fair skin tones and freckles.** Their fair skin often makes them prone to sunburn. **Scientists have a theory that the color adaptation has something to do with the fact that Scotland and Ireland have lots of dark and rainy weather.**

Instant Genius
The mythological unicorn is the national animal of Scotland.

#81

Which animals are older:

sharks or
dinosaurs?

a. Sharks

b. Dinosaurs

c. It's a tie.

Goblin shark

NOW YOU KNOW!
Some shark species, such as the goblin shark, have existed for more than 100 million years and are considered living fossils.

ANSWER: **a** sharks

Instant Genius
The oldest species still living on Earth is the horseshoe crab.

ACCORDING TO SCIENTISTS, SHARKS HAVE BEEN AROUND FOR ABOUT 450 MILLION YEARS. Sharks' first ancestors were alive when coral reefs were first forming on the planet during the late Ordovician period. Dinosaurs came around 220 million years later, during the Triassic period. Many of these ancient sharks were much bigger than they are today. In fact, about 23 million years ago the world's biggest shark was swimming through Earth's oceans. **The megalodon is the biggest fish that ever lived. It was up to 60 feet (18 m) long, about the size of a school bus!**

Where did **pasta** originate?

a. Europe

b. Asia

c. North America

Instant Genius

A single strand of spaghetti is called a spaghetto.

ANSWER: b Asia

WHILE SOME PEOPLE TODAY ASSOCIATE PASTA WITH ITALY, THE NOODLE IS BELIEVED TO HAVE COME FROM CENTRAL ASIA, WHERE IT WAS FIRST EATEN THOUSANDS OF YEARS AGO. Archaeologists aren't sure exactly how noodles got to Europe, but once the food arrived in areas near the Mediterranean Sea, the ingredients changed to create the pasta we know today, which is a mixture of wheat flour, eggs, and water. **Thomas Jefferson is thought to have helped make pasta popular in America.** After enjoying it in Paris, France, while visiting there, he brought pasta back home with him.

The human body's
largest protein
has a very short name.

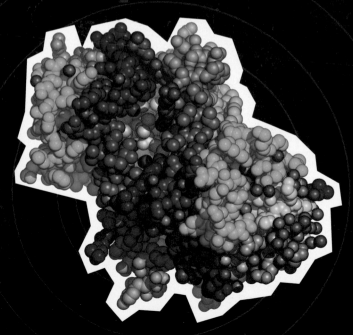

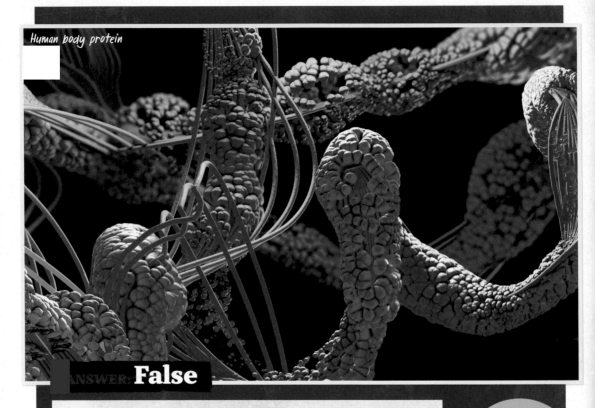

Human body protein

ANSWER: False

THE LARGEST KNOWN PROTEIN IN THE HUMAN BODY ALSO HAS THE LONGEST NAME IN THE ENGLISH LANGUAGE. The protein, which is found in muscle, was first discovered in 1977 and named two years later. The full chemical name contains a whopping 189,819 letters and takes more than three hours to pronounce. Why is it so long? **Proteins are named by citing all of the amino acids inside them.** Since this protein is the biggest, with 27,000 amino acids, it has the most chemicals to include in its name. Scientists refer to the protein by a shorter name: titin.

NOW YOU KNOW!
Hippopotomonstroses-quippedaliophobia is the fear of long words.

What was **Alexander Hamilton** famous for?

a. starring in a Broadway play

b. inventing the light bulb

c. being the first secretary of the U.S. Treasury

ANSWER: **c**

being the first secretary of the U.S. Treasury

ALEXANDER HAMILTON WAS BORN POOR IN THE BRITISH WEST INDIES. In 1772, he made his way to colonial America and became a big supporter of George Washington. He rose through the ranks during the Revolutionary War. **As one of America's Founding Fathers, Hamilton believed in a strong central government.** He was passionate about the U.S. Constitution and co-authored the Federalist Papers, which was a series of 85 essays urging others to accept and support the Constitution. **As the first secretary of the U.S. Treasury, Hamilton led the country's first financial practices.** He was killed in a duel in 1804 by a political foe, Aaron Burr.

Instant Genius
Hamilton was banned from going to school because his parents never got married.

Bananas
are radioactive.

#85

ANSWER: **True**

BANANAS ARE, IN FACT, RADIOACTIVE. Everything, and everyone, in the world is made up of teeny-tiny atoms. When certain atoms break apart, they give off something called radiation. In large doses, radiation can cause cancer and can even be lethal. Bananas naturally contain an element called potassium. A teeny-tiny fraction of potassium's atoms are radioactive. **But never fear. You would have to eat a lot of bananas for the radiation to affect you.** So go right ahead and eat that banana split! You'll be doing your body a favor: **Potassium helps the body regulate fluid balance, helps your muscles work, and prevents bone loss and even kidney stones.**

Instant Genius
As a banana ripens, it gets more nutritious.

ANSWER: **True**

NOT ALL CLAMS LIVE AS LONG AS 500 YEARS, BUT A QUAHOG CLAM FOUND OFF THE COAST OF ICELAND DID LIVE THAT LONG. HOW? Scientists say that the **clam's long life was due to a very low metabolism** as a result of living in the very cold waters of the North Atlantic Ocean. **The clam, which scientists named Ming, was found off the coast of Iceland in 2006 and its actual age was determined to be 507.**

Instant Genius
The largest natural pearl ever found was reported to be worth more than 100 million dollars.

If you added up all of the gifts given in the song **"The Twelve Days of Christmas,"** what would be the total?

THE
TWELVE DAYS
OF
CHRISTMAS.
Sung at King Pepin's Ball.

THE first day of Christmas,
My true love sent to me
A partridge in a pear-tree.

a. 12

b. 20

c. 364

ANSWER: C 364

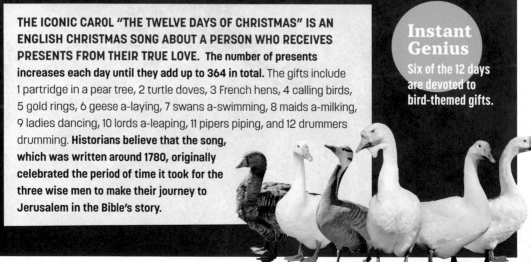

THE ICONIC CAROL "THE TWELVE DAYS OF CHRISTMAS" IS AN ENGLISH CHRISTMAS SONG ABOUT A PERSON WHO RECEIVES PRESENTS FROM THEIR TRUE LOVE. **The number of presents increases each day until they add up to 364 in total.** The gifts include 1 partridge in a pear tree, 2 turtle doves, 3 French hens, 4 calling birds, 5 gold rings, 6 geese a-laying, 7 swans a-swimming, 8 maids a-milking, 9 ladies dancing, 10 lords a-leaping, 11 pipers piping, and 12 drummers drumming. **Historians believe that the song, which was written around 1780, originally celebrated the period of time it took for the three wise men to make their journey to Jerusalem in the Bible's story.**

Instant Genius
Six of the 12 days are devoted to bird-themed gifts.

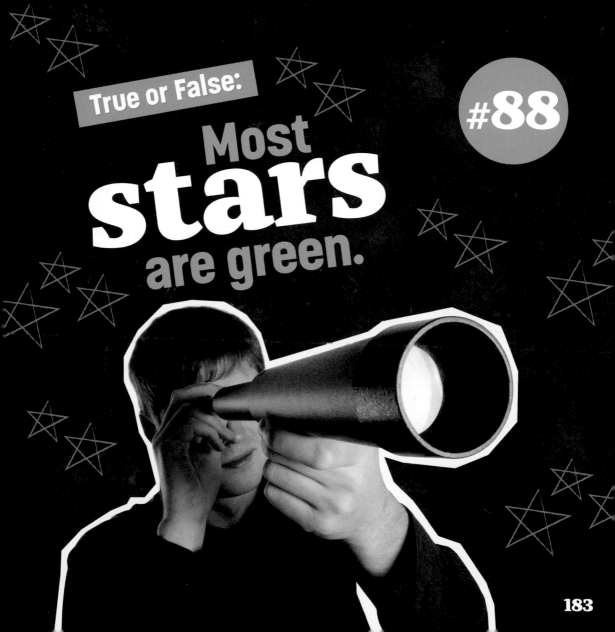

ANSWER: **False**

STARS GLOW ACCORDING TO THE HEAT THEY PRODUCE. **A star's color is determined by its temperature.** Stars burn in a range of temperatures. Each temperature has a corresponding color. **The hottest stars are blue and the coolest stars are red.** Stars on the temperature spectrum between blue and red can appear white, yellow, and orange. **Stars never appear green to our eyes because the color green is so close to the middle of the spectrum that the combination of colors appears white to our eyes.**

Instant Genius

The coolest stars are still scorching hot. They are about 5,000° F (2,760° C)!

Which
dog breed has
been the most popular in
the United States for the
last several decades?

#89

a. the poodle

c. the Labrador retriever

b. the golden retriever

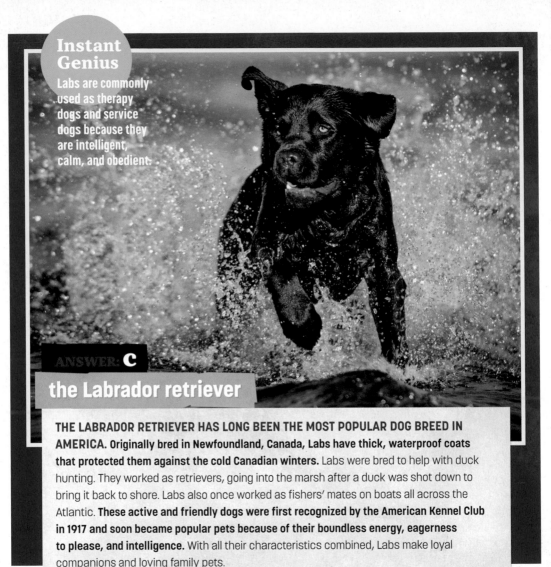

ANSWER: **C**

the Labrador retriever

THE LABRADOR RETRIEVER HAS LONG BEEN THE MOST POPULAR DOG BREED IN AMERICA. Originally bred in Newfoundland, Canada, Labs have thick, waterproof coats that protected them against the cold Canadian winters. Labs were bred to help with duck hunting. They worked as retrievers, going into the marsh after a duck was shot down to bring it back to shore. Labs also once worked as fishers' mates on boats all across the Atlantic. **These active and friendly dogs were first recognized by the American Kennel Club in 1917 and soon became popular pets because of their boundless energy, eagerness to please, and intelligence.** With all their characteristics combined, Labs make loyal companions and loving family pets.

90

True or False:

Vegetarians can eat

Jell-O

for dessert.

THOUGH IT MAY NOT SEEM LIKE IT, JELL-O IS MADE FROM ANIMAL PRODUCTS. The active ingredient in the brightly colored, jiggly dish is gelatin, which is the same stuff that's in gummy bears and marshmallows. **Gelatin is a protein from the tendons, ligaments, and bones of animals like cows and pigs. It can also come from pigskin.** Once it's extracted, it's dried and ground into a powder. When boiling water is added to the powder, it breaks down the bonds that hold the gelatin together. **This causes the proteins to float around. Once you put Jell-O in the refrigerator, the cold temperature causes the gelatin to come back together into a jiggly jelly.**

NOW YOU KNOW! Salt Lake City, Utah, U.S.A., is the Jell-O capital of the world. Utah residents eat twice as much Jell-O as the rest of the world.

Instant Genius
There's a Jell-O museum in Le Roy, New York, where you can see all kinds of Jell-O memorabilia.

Don't get too close!

ANSWER: True

JUST AS EVERYONE HAS A UNIQUE FINGERPRINT, EACH HUMAN ALSO HAS A SIGNATURE SCENT CALLED AN ODORTYPE. **Odortypes are genetic, which means we inherit them from our parents.** Chemical molecules in the fluids we give off, like sweat and urine, transmit our particular scent. **Our odortypes can change slightly depending on the food we eat, but the base of each person's particular scent is as permanent as our fingerprints.** And scientists have found something interesting when it comes to identical twins: **The acids in the body odor of identical twins is about 10 times more similar than that of people who are not identical twins.**

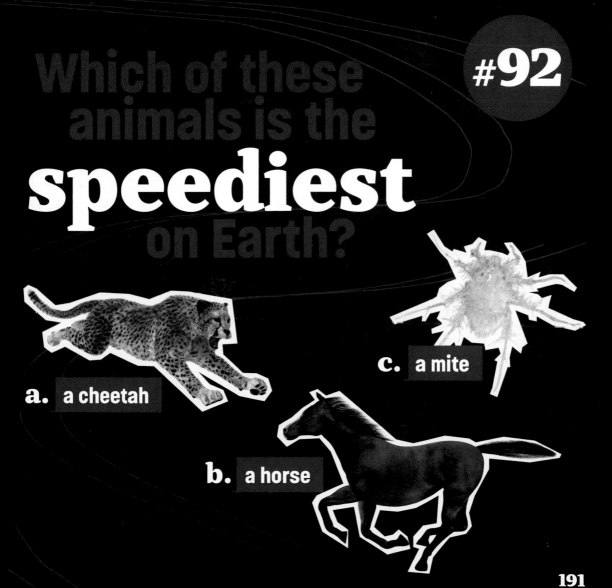

THE CALIFORNIA MITE CAN MOVE ABOUT 1 FOOT (30 CM) PER SECOND. This may not seem like much, but this little creature is only about the size of a sesame seed! **In that one second time frame, the mite moves a distance of 322 body lengths.** When comparing that to the world's fastest human, Usain Bolt, it's the equivalent of Bolt moving at a speed of 1,300 miles an hour (2,100 kmh). Bolt's actual top speed is recorded at about 45 miles an hour (72 kmh). **These mites are so fast that scientists had to use high-speed photography just to be able to record their movement.**

NOW YOU KNOW!
The Australian tiger beetle is the fasted running insect, moving up to 5.5 miles an hour (9 kmh). This means in one second it can move 120 times the length of its body!

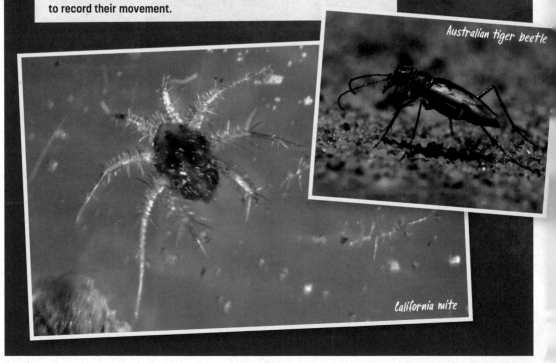

Australian tiger beetle

California mite

How much ice is Earth losing each year?

a. 1.3 million tons

b. 1.3 billion tons

c. 1.3 trillion tons

193

Perito Moreno Glacier, Patagonia, Argentina

ANSWER: C

1.3 trillion tons

ACCORDING TO SCIENTISTS, EARTH'S ICE IS MELTING FASTER THAN IT WAS 30 YEARS AGO. Why? Greenhouse gases, such as carbon dioxide released from cars and power plants, are trapping heat within Earth's atmosphere. **This is causing changes in Earth's climate conditions.** One consequence of these changes is that glacier ice and ice sheets are melting faster, the same way ice cubes melt faster on a hot day. Melting ice means that our sea levels are rising, causing increased flooding. **Climate change is also responsible for stronger and more damaging hurricanes, as well as more wildfires.**

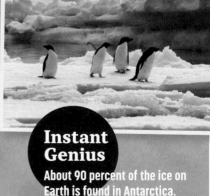

Instant Genius

About 90 percent of the ice on Earth is found in Antarctica.

When was **money** invented?

a. 100 years ago

c. 5,000 years ago

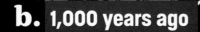

b. 1,000 years ago

ANSWER: **C**

5,000 years ago

THE EARLIEST KNOWN FORM OF MONEY WAS THE SHEKEL, WHICH WAS USED 5,000 YEARS AGO IN AN AREA OF WESTERN ASIA THAT WAS KNOWN AS MESOPOTAMIA. **The first mints, which are places where money is made, created silver and gold coins to pay armies.** Even before there were coins and bills, people used the things they had in order to pay for what they wanted. For example, hunters traded tools and weapons. **People also started using rare items found in nature, such as pieces of gold, silver, and other precious metals. Shells were also traded in some places. Cows, salt, cacao beans, and other spices were used as currency, too.**

British pound

When your cat puts its **rear end** in your face, what is it trying to say?

a. "I don't like you."

b. "I love you."

c. "Who are you?"

Do you hear me?

NOW YOU KNOW!
Direct eye contact and a twitchy tail held high in the air, or a tail draping over your legs, are also cat language for friendship.

ANSWER: b "I love you."

CATS IDENTIFY EACH OTHER BY SCENT. **The act of presenting a tail to your face is an instinctive behavior from a happy kittenhood. When your cat was a kitten, its mother licked all of its body parts—including the rear end—to keep the kitten clean.** When your cat puts its behind in your face now, it could be reaffirming the bond it had with its mother. Cats have many different ways of displaying affection. **Another is kneading—when a cat gently pushes its paws back and forth into you.** This is the same thing that the kitten did to get milk from its mother. **Other signs of affection include your cat headbutting you, or rubbing its chin against you.** Your feline is marking you as "theirs" by using the scent glands on their cheeks and head to announce, "Hands off, this is MY person."

#96

The longest reigning monarch in the United Kingdom was

Queen Victoria.

Instant Genius

Throughout her life, Queen Elizabeth II has had Welsh corgis as beloved pets.

Welsh corgi

ANSWER: **False**

ON SEPTEMBER 9, 2015, QUEEN ELIZABETH II SURPASSED QUEEN VICTORIA'S RECORD OF 63 YEARS AND 216 DAYS ON THE THRONE TO BECOME THE LONGEST REIGNING MONARCH OF THE UNITED KINGDOM. **Queen Elizabeth assumed the throne in 1953 at the age of 27, after her father died.** Since then, she has had four children and is now a grandmother and great-grandmother. Because of her long reign, Queen Elizabeth is the most well-traveled British monarch in history, having traveled all over the world. **In 2012, Queen Elizabeth had her Diamond Jubilee, which celebrated 60 years on the throne.**

True or False:

Jupiter's Great Red Spot
is actually a large desert.

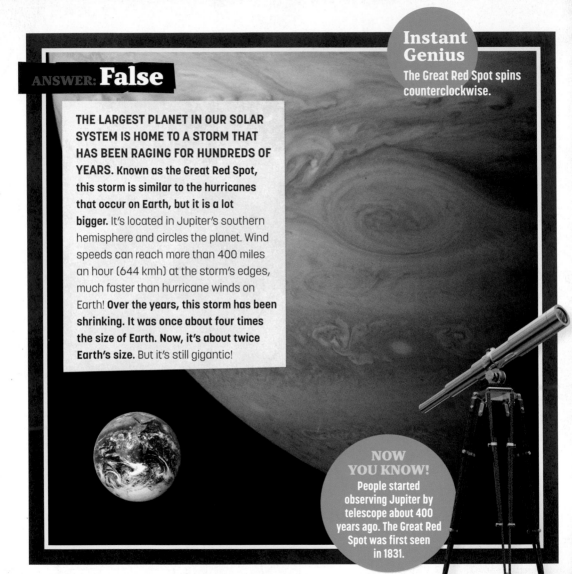

ANSWER: **False**

THE LARGEST PLANET IN OUR SOLAR SYSTEM IS HOME TO A STORM THAT HAS BEEN RAGING FOR HUNDREDS OF YEARS. Known as the Great Red Spot, this storm is similar to the hurricanes that occur on Earth, but it is a lot **bigger.** It's located in Jupiter's southern hemisphere and circles the planet. Wind speeds can reach more than 400 miles an hour (644 kmh) at the storm's edges, much faster than hurricane winds on Earth! **Over the years, this storm has been shrinking. It was once about four times the size of Earth. Now, it's about twice Earth's size.** But it's still gigantic!

American cheese

was invented in America.

Swiss cheese

ANSWER: False

AMERICAN CHEESE WAS INVENTED IN SWITZERLAND IN 1911. Swiss cheese makers took a hard Swiss cheese and added a preservative called sodium citrate that made it softer and longer-lasting. They wanted to create a cheese with a longer shelf life so that it could be shipped around the world without spoiling. Around the same time, a Canadian-born cheese maker was experimenting with shredded cheddar and Colby and remelting them to make a sliceable cheese that would last long and could be shipped to soldiers during war. He patented the process in 1916, and we've been eating sliced cheese ever since.

colby cheese

#99

One of the **strongest muscles** in your body is located in your jaw.

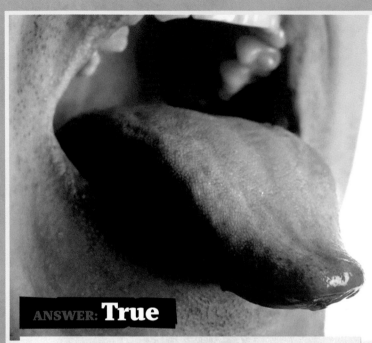

ANSWER: True

IN THE HUMAN JAW THERE IS A SMALL MUSCLE CALLED THE MASSETER. If you clench your teeth and touch your cheek, you can actually feel your masseter flex. **Located at the hinge of the jaw, the muscle is responsible for helping us clench and chew, and it is considered one of the strongest muscles in the body because of the pressure it can exert.** Pressure is the amount of force something can give off over a certain area. **Usually, the masseter muscle can chomp down with a whopping 200 pounds (90 kg) of force onto your molar teeth.** But the strongest bite ever recorded by a human was done with a force of 975 pounds (422 kg)!

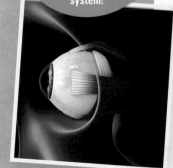

In the **Middle Ages,** what was the first step to becoming a knight?

a. becoming a page

b. becoming a squire

c. becoming a guard

ANSWER: a **becoming a page**

IN THE MIDDLE AGES, KNIGHTS USUALLY HELD HIGH STATUS IN SOCIETY. The journey to get there, however, was not glamorous. **The first step started around the age of 7, when a boy left home to become a page.** Pages were required to do chores and learn skills such as how to handle weapons. **When a page turned 14 years old, he became a squire, an assistant who helped a knight dress in his battle armor.** Squires also learned about weaponry and how to attack enemies while on horseback. **Between the ages of 18 and 21, a squire was knighted if he had acquired the skills and manners to deem him worthy enough to become a knight.**

NOW YOU KNOW!

A knight's suit of armor was made of iron and steel. The full suit weighed 5 to 55 pounds (20–25 kg).

Great white sharks
are silent.

101

Boo!

Knock, knock!

ANSWER: True

WHALES, DOLPHINS, SHRIMP, AND MOST OTHER FISH PRODUCE SONGS, GRUNTS, SQUAWKS, OR SOME KIND OF SOUND. BUT GREAT WHITES DO NOT VOCALIZE IN ANY WAY. **Not only do they lack vocal chords, they don't even make noise when they swim!** Their scales are so aerodynamic that great whites can slip through the water without a sound. To communicate, they use body language. **Great whites will move their heads, open their jaws, arch their bodies, and use slapping displays to "tell" a rival to back off when competing for the same prey.**

Instant Genius

While still in their mother's womb, great white sharks swallow their teeth.

**Spot the
7 Random
Differences!**

Turn to page 215 for the answers.

211

Index

Page numbers in *italic* refer to images.

Photo Credits

The publishers would like to thank the following for the use of their images. While every effort has been made to credit images, the publishers will be pleased to correct any errors or omissions in future editions of the book.

t = top; b = bottom; l = left; r = right; c = center

Alamy: pp. 20(br), 21(tr), 27(cr), 28(t), 32, 48(br), 49, 54(t), 62(t), 67, 70(t), 72(t), 78, 82(t), 92(t), 100, 104(t,br), 116, 127, 128(t,br), 129(cr), 130, 140(bl), 144(t), 146(bl), 152, 154, 163, 166(t,cr), 170(t), 173, 176, 184, 188, 199, 208(t).

Dreamstime: pp. 1, 2(br), 4, 5, 6, 7, 8–9, 10(tl,br), 11, 13, 14, 15, 16(t,br), 17, 18, 21(bc,br), 22, 23, 24(main image,br), 25(bl,bc,br), 26(t,br), 27(bl,bc), 28(br), 29, 30(bl), 31, 33(bl,br), 34(t,bl), 35, 36(t,br), 37, 38(t,br), 39(tr,cr,br), 40(bl,r), 41(tc,tr,bl,br), 42, 44(tl,tc,tr,br), 45(cl,cr,bc), 46, 47, 48(t), 50(t,br), 51, 52, 53(bl,br), 54(bl), 55, 56(t,br), 58(tr), 59(bl,r), 60(t,bl), 61, 62(br), 63, 64, 65, 67, 68, 69, 70(br), 71, 72(br), 73(bl,br), 74, 75, 76(t,br), 77, 79(cl,cr,bc), 80, 81(l,c,r), 82(br), 83, 84(bl,r), 85, 86, 87(cl,cr,bc), 88(t), 89, 90(t,br), 91, 93, 94(t), 95, 96(br), 97(bl,br), 98(t,br), 99(cl,cr,bc), 101, 102(br), 103, 105, 106(t,br), 107(t,cr), 108, 109, 110(stamp,candy), 113, 114, 115, 117, 118(t), 119, 120(t,br), 121, 122, 123, 124, 125, 129(cl,c), 131(cr,bl,bc,br), 132 (tl,main image,br), 134(bl), 135, 136(t,br), 137, 138, 140(r), 141, 142, 143, 144(br), 145(l), 147, 148, 149, 150(t,br), 151(cl,c), 153, 155, 156(t,cr), 157, 158(br), 159, 160(t), 163, 164(t,br), 165(cl,cr,bc), 167(l,c,r), 168(t,cr), 169(tr,bl), 170(bl), 171, 172(t,br), 174, 175, 177, 178, 179, 180(t,br), 182(t,br), 183, 185(bl,bc,br), 186, 187, 189, 190, 191(cl,br), 193, 194(t,br), 195(cl,bc), 196(t,br), 197, 198, 200(main image,cr), 202(br), 203, 204(t), 205, 206(t,br), 207, 208(cr), 209, 210, 211(t,b), 215.

Getty Images: pp. 10(tr), 12(b), 57, 58(tl), 102(t), 110(t), 133, 192(cr).

iStockphoto: pp. 53(runners), 66, 160(br), 195(cr), 204(br).

Library of Congress, Washington, D.C.: pp. 88(br), 139(bc,br), 151(cr).

Metropolitan Museum of Art, New York: p. 12(tc).

NASA (National Aeronautics and Space Administration): pp. 2(tl), 19, 20(t), 96(t), 111(bl,bc,br), 112, 126(t), 145(r), 146(t), 158(t), 161, 162, 201, 202(main image).

National Gallery of Art, Washington, D.C.: p. 12(tr).

National Library of Medicine, Maryland: p. 92(br).

Nature Picture Library: p. 94(br).

The New Bremen Pumpkinfest Committee: p. 30(t).

Science Photo Library: pp. 43, 126(cr).

Shutterstock: p. 214.

Wikimedia Commons: pp. 118(br), 134(r), 181.

Grace C. Wu and Jonathan C. Wright: pp. 191(cr), 192(bl).

Credits

Text and cover design copyright © 2022 by
Penguin Random House LLC

Visit us on the Web! **rhcbooks.com**

Educators and librarians, for a variety of teaching tools, visit us
at **RHTeachersLibrarians.com**

Library of Congress Cataloging-in-Publication Data is available
upon request.
ISBN 978-0-593-45050-5 (trade)
ISBN 978-0-593-45052-9 (lib. bdg.)
ISBN 978-0-593-51614-0 (ebook)

COVER PHOTO CREDITS:
Front Cover Photo: Shutterstock
Back Cover Photo: Dreamstime

MANUFACTURED IN ITALY
10 9 8 7 6 5 4 3 2 1
First Edition

Produced by Fun Factory Press, LLC, in association with
Potomac Global Media, LLC.

The publisher would like to thank the following people for their
contributions to this book: Melina Gerosa Bellows, President,
Fun Factory Press, and Series Creator and Author; Priyanka
Lamichhane, Editor and Project Manager; Chad Tomlinson, Art
Director; Jen Agresta, Copy Editor; Michelle Harris, Fact-checker;
Potomac Global Media: Kevin Mulroy, Publisher; Barbara Brownell
Grogan, Editor in Chief, Christopher L. Mazzatenta, Designer;
Susannah Jayes and Ellen Dupont, Picture Researchers; Jane
Sunderland and Heather McElwain, Contributing Editors